The Cook's Pocket Bible

The Cook's Pocket Bible

Every culinary rule of thumb at your fingertips

Roni **JAY**

Editor Richard Craze

WHITE LADDER PRESS

new tricks for old dogs

Published by White Ladder Press Ltd
Great Ambrook, Near Ipplepen, Devon TQ12 5UL
01803 813343
www.whiteladderpress.com

First published in Great Britain in 2006

10 9 8 7 6 5 4 3 2 1

10-digit ISBN 1 905410 09 3
13-digit ISBN 978 1 905410 09 5

British Library Cataloguing in Publication Data
A CIP record for this book can be obtained from the British Library.

Designed and typeset by Julie Martin Ltd
Cover design by Julie Martin Ltd
Cover photographs by Jonathon Bosley
Additional illustrations by Chris Mutter
Cover printed by St Austell Printing Company
Printed and bound by TJ International Ltd, Padstow, Cornwall

 White Ladder books are distributed in the UK by Virgin Books

White Ladder Press
Great Ambrook, Near Ipplepen, Devon TQ12 5UL
01803 813343
www.whiteladderpress.com

Acknowledgements

I would like to thank my father, Tony Jay, for his excellent help with the wine section of this book. My lack of enthusiasm for drinking fine wines must be a great disappointment to him. However he has never complained, and generously and resignedly consumes my share for me.

I would also like to thank chef Matthew Lamb for reading through the entire manuscript for me to make sure that it all met with his professional approval, and for adding a couple of clever tips that I hadn't known about (such as how to peel a kiwi fruit).

Contents

Fish and seafood ⟍

Vegetables, fruit and nuts 53

Pasta, pulses, rice and grains
72

Christmas

*Classic recipes you need
to check* ━━◗ 159

Index   168

Introduction

The milk is about to boil over, your guests are turning up in half an hour, the oven timer has just gone off, and you're damned if you can find the answer to a simple question. What are the quantities for a crumble mixture? Or can you put the skin of this fancy fruit you've bought into the fruit salad? Or is it OK to serve this cheese to a pregnant guest?

The Cook's Pocket Bible is here for all those moments. And even when you're not in quite such a rush, it can be impossible to find out what you want elsewhere. Can you freeze hard boiled eggs? How long will this joint take to cook? What does the American recipe you're using mean when it says 'heavy cream'? That's why I've brought together all the information into one book. It's not a cookery book – it's full of useful information for novice cooks but it doesn't contain instructions. You have recipe books for that. This book contains the supporting information that you won't find in the recipe book.

As the subtitle of this book indicates, it contains plenty of rules of thumb. These can be extremely useful – especially in the absence of more specific information – however since I don't know the vagaries of your personal taste, or the idosyncracies of your particular oven, I can't guarantee that every one of them will hold true every time. Nevertheless, most of them will work for you most of the time, and those that don't shouldn't be far off. If you've lost the instruction book, or the recipe doesn't tell you what you want to know, or your meat came from the butcher without the fancy labelling you get in supermarkets, this book will be exactly what you need.

Charts and tables

☙— *Weights and measures* —❧

Because exact equivalents of weights and measures involve unnecessary decimal points that you don't want to bother with, conversions are always approximate. As some cookery writers round up and some round down, they don't always tally with each other. So the chart here is as accurate as others, but not necessarily identical. The important thing is to make sure that you use the same version throughout any given recipe.

OUNCES/POUNDS TO GRAMS/KILOS ●—▶

$1/_4$oz	5g	9oz	225g
$1/_2$oz	10g	10oz	250g
1oz	25g	11oz	275g
2oz	50g	12oz	300g
3oz	75g	13oz	325g
4oz	100g	14oz	350g
5oz	125g	15oz	375g
6oz	150g	1 lb	400g
7oz	175g	$1^1/_2$ lb	700g
8oz	200g	2 lb	900g

Rule of thumb

A flat tablespoon of sugar weighs an ounce.
A rounded tablespoon of flour weighs an ounce.
1 tablespoon is equivalent to 3 teaspoons.

PINTS TO ML/LITRES ➝

$^1/_4$ pt	125ml
$^1/_2$ pt	250ml
$^3/_4$ pt	375ml
1 pt	500ml ($^1/_2$ litre)
$1^1/_2$ pt	750ml
2 pt	1 litre

Rule of thumb

A pint of water weighs a pound and three quarters.

SPOONS TO ML ➝

1 teaspoon	5 ml
1 dessertspoon	10 ml
1 tablespoon	15 ml

CUPS TO ML TO FLUID OUNCES TO ➝
TABLESPOONS

cups	mls	fl oz	tablespoons
$^1/_8$ cup	30ml	1 fl oz	2
$^1/_4$ cup	60ml	2 fl oz	4
$^1/_3$ cup	80ml	2.5 fl oz	5 + 1 teaspoon
$^1/_2$ cup	125ml	4 fl oz	8

$^2/_3$ cup	160 ml	5 fl oz	10 + 2 teaspoons
$^3/_4$ cup	190ml	6 fl oz	12
1 cup	250ml	8 fl oz	16
2 cups	500ml	1 pint	32

Rule of thumb
A pinch (if in doubt) is less than $^1/_2$ teaspoon.
A dash is a few drops (sorry I can't be more specific).

Oven conversion chart

I've included range cooker ovens here as I feel sorry for them – they usually get left out. If you own one, however, you'll know that they all have their own personalities, and this is therefore only a rough guide.

	Gas regulo	°C	°F	4 oven range	2 oven range
Very slow	$^1/_4$	110	225	Warming	Lower bottom
	$^1/_2$	130	250		
	1	140	275	Simmering	
Slow middle	2	150	300		Lower
	3	160	325		
Moderate	4	180	350	Baking	Lower top
	5	190	375		Upper bottom
	6	200	400		

Hot	7	220	425	Roasting	Upper middle
	8	230	450		
Very hot	9	250	475	Upper top	

Rule of thumb
If you have a fan oven, you need to reduce the recommended temperature by about 20°C.

❧— *Temperature charts* —❧

ROAST MEAT ━●

If you use a meat thermometer you should always insert it into the thickest part of the meat, and keep it away from any bones. These temperatures are for roast joints or whole roast birds.

		°C	°F
Beef and lamb	Rare	60	140
	Medium	70	160
	Well done	80	175
Pork	Medium	75	170
	Well done	80	175
Poultry		80	175

SUGAR SYRUPS

If you make syrups, caramels and toffees you probably have a sugar thermometer. Here's a quick reminder of the temperatures for different stages.

Syrup	°C	°F
Coating syrup	100	212
Small thread	103–105	217–221
Large thread	106–110	223–230
Small pearl	110–112	230–234
Large pearl	113–115	235–239
Soft ball	116–125	241–257
Hard ball	126–135	259–275
Soft crack	136–140	277–284
Hard crack	146–155	295–311
Light caramel	156–165	313–329
Dark caramel	166–175	331–347

Chef's tip

If you don't have an oil thermometer to test the temperature of oil when you're deep frying, here's a quick way to gauge the temperature without one. Drop a cube of white bread into the oil and time how long it takes to brown evenly. As a rough guide:

20 seconds: 382–390°F
40 seconds: 365–382°F
60 seconds: 350–365°F

US and British cooking terms

If you're using a recipe from an American book, it's easy to get confused by directions to add heavy cream, or to use fava beans when you've no idea where to get hold of them. So here are a few of the most common translations you might need.

US	British
Beet	Beetroot
Broil	Grill
Confectioners' sugar	Icing sugar
Corn starch	Cornflour
Eggplant	Aubergine
Fava bean	Broad bean
Golden raisins	Sultanas
Green bean	French bean
Ground meat	Mince
Half & half	Single cream & milk
Heavy cream	Double cream
Light cream	Single cream
Molasses	Treacle
Seeded	Stoned
Superfine granulated	Caster sugar
Variety meats	Offal
Zucchini	Courgette

Glossary of cooking terms

There are countless words associated with cooking and serving food, including terms for different kinds of cooking equipment, various types of dishes and so on. However, I assume you already know what you're cooking, and you can use a saucepan without necessarily knowing its name. So I've restricted this glossary to words which you might easily encounter while following a recipe and want reassurance that they mean what you think they do.

Al dente Italian for 'to the tooth', this means the food is tender but still has a firmness in the middle.

Bain-marie A double boiler pan, either purpose made or cobbled together by putting a pan of water on the heat with another pan or dish inside it. Used to keep the contents of the inner pan away from direct heat.

Baste To spoon cooking juices (usually fat) over something while it's cooking.

Bind To use a liquid, often beaten egg, to get dry ingredients to hold together.

Blanch Apart from how you react to certain recipe instructions, this means to plunge briefly into boiling water. This helps to retain colour, loosen skins for peeling (eg tomatoes), soften, parcook (culinary speak for part cook) or remove strong flavours.

Blind baking To cook a pastry case without the filling. It's filled with dried beans to keep its shape, which are then removed after baking.

Blitz To blend with an electric mixer.

Braise To cook very slowly, in a small amount of liquid, in a pan with a tight fitting lid.

Caramelise To cook sugar until brown, or to brown the sugar topping on a dish such as crème brulée.

Chiffonade Fine shreds, usually of lettuce or other green vegetables such as spinach, made by flattening the leaves on top of each other, rolling tightly and then cutting into strips.

Clarify To make clear, as you'd imagine, but in this case literally: to remove any cloudiness or sediment from stock, consommé, jelly or melted butter.

Cream To beat fat and sugar together until light.

Croûte A slice of toasted or fried bried on which food is served.

Croûtons Small cubes of bread fried until crisp and brown, generally used as a garnish for salads and soups.

Deglaze To rinse out a pan with liquid such as stock or wine in order to collect the sediment to use in a sauce.

Degrease Sounds revoltingly Dickensian. Actually it means to skim off the fat from the surface of a liquid.

Eggwash Egg beaten together with a little water or milk to brush over food before cooking to brown it during baking.

Flake To break food into natural segments, particularly used to apply to cooked fish.

Fold To combine two lots of ingredients gently with a metal spoon to keep their lightness. Usually one of them is beaten egg white, which would deflate if stirred.

Glaze To give a shiny coat. Used with sweet dishes this generally means to coat with melted apricot jam, using a brush. With vegetables, such as glazed carrots, it usually means coated with melted butter.

Hull To remove the green calyx (where the stem meets the fruit) from fruit such as strawberries and tomatoes.

Infuse To steep in hot liquid in order to transfer flavour to the liquid.

Julienne Vegetables cut into very fine strips.

Knead To work dough.

Knock back To knead the air out of dough after it has risen.

Lard This is animal fat, of course, as a noun. As a verb, however, it means to insert strips of fat into meat.

Lardons Strips or cubes of thick streaky bacon.

Marinade Liquid in which food is marinated (see below).

Marinate To leave something to steep in a flavoured liquid.

Parboil To boil until partly cooked.

Parcook To partly cook (usually by parboiling – see above entry – but not necessarily).

Pare To trim or peel.

Prove To allow dough to rest somewhere warm while it rises.

Purée To blend, mash or sieve until smooth.

Reduce To make a liquid more concentrated by boiling it until some of it has evaporated.

Refresh To put a food under cold running water to cool it down.

Ribbon stage The stage when whisking sauce, cream or egg yolk when it falls from the whisk back into the bowl in a thick stream that remains visible on the surface for a few seconds before folding in on itself. In other words that point where it is barely either solid or liquid.

Roux Flour and fat cooked together to form the basis, and thickening agent, for a sauce.

Rub in To rub fat and flour together between thumb and fingers until it is the consistency of fine bread-crumbs.

Sabayon Egg yolks whisked with liquid until foamy.

Sauté To shallow fry quickly in hot fat.

Scald To heat liquid, usually milk, to just below boiling point. Or, obviously, to spill boiling liquid on yourself (though you won't find this instruction in many recipes).

Score To make regular cuts in the surface of meat or fish before cooking. Pork crackling is the obvious example.

Seal To cook the outside of a piece of meat in a hot pan or oven, before the main cooking process.

Sear To cook quickly on both sides in hot fat.

Shred To cut in fine strips.

Skim To remove scum or fat from the surface of a liquid using a slotted spoon or an old-fashioned skimmer (like a flat ladle with holes in it).

Sweat Not you standing over a hot stove, but the food: to cook in fat with a lid on the pan so the food doesn't dis-colour. Most often applied to onions at the start of a recipe.

Velouté A basic sauce made from a roux with liquid added gradually.

Zest The outer, coloured skin of citrus fruit without the bitter pith beneath.

Meat

— Roasting times —

Joint	How well done	Minutes per lb/400g
Beef	Rare	15 minutes per lb + 15 minutes
	Medium	20 minutes per lb + 20 minutes
	Well done	25 minutes per lb + 25 minutes
Lamb	Rare	15 minutes per lb + 15 minutes
	Medium	20 minutes per lb + 20 minutes
	Well done	25 minutes per lb + 25 minutes
Pork	Medium	25 minutes per lb + 25 minutes
	Well done	30 minutes per lb + 30 minutes
Veal		25 minutes per lb + 25 minutes
Venison		20 minutes per lb + 20 minutes

Rule of thumb
Roast red meat at 220°C/425°F/Gas mark 7/middle of the roasting oven for the first 15–20 minutes to sear the outside of the joint. Then reduce the temperature to 180°C/350°F/Gas mark 4/bottom of roasting oven for the rest of the cooking time.

For meat thermometer temperatures to see if the joint is cooked, see page 6.

●— *Portion sizes* —●

Is that cut of meat you've got going to go round? Here's a rule of thumb guide to how much meat to allow per person by weight (of the meat, that is, not the person).

Portion	Off the bone	On the bone
Respectable	4oz/100g	6oz/150g
Generous	6oz/150g	9oz/225g
For the very hungry	8oz/200g	12oz/300g

●— *Traditional accompaniments* —●

You don't have to serve these, of course, but here's a quick reminder if you want it of the traditional accompaniments to roast joints, as well as gravy.

Meat	Accompaniments
Beef	Yorkshire pudding, horseradish sauce
Gammon	Pease pudding, parsley sauce
Lamb	Mint sauce or mint jelly, redcurrant jelly
Pork	Apple sauce, sage and onion stuffing
Venison	Fruit jelly: rowanberry, damson, redcurrant

— *Beef* —

RECOGNISING GOOD BEEF

If you're not sure how fresh or how good your beef is, here are the signs of good quality meat you should look for:

- the smell shouldn't be strong
- the lean meat should be bright to dark red, and flecked with fat
- the fat should be a slightly creamy colour, firm and brittle
- the meat shouldn't be too moist
- it should never be slimy, discoloured or smelly

CUTS AND HOW TO COOK THEM

If you've bought a nice looking piece of beef – or just the only one you could get at the price – you might not have had a meal in mind at the time. You might want to decide how to cook it when the time comes. Well, now it's time to decide and – to help you make up your mind – here's a quick guide to the generally recommended cooking method for different cuts of beef.

Cut	Best cooking method
Brisket	Cook long and slow, eg braise or pot roast
Fillet	Roast, or cut into steaks to grill or fry
Minced beef	Burgers, meatballs and meat sauce
Ribs	Roast on the bone
Rump	Braise whole, or cut into steaks to grill or fry
Silverside	Slow cook, eg boil, braise or pot roast

Sirloin	Roast or cut into steaks to grill or fry
Stewing steak	You guess
Topside	Pot roast or braise (you can roast it but watch it doesn't dry out)

HOW TO TELL WHEN IT'S COOKED ●━━▶

You can use a meat thermometer of course, and your beef should be 60–80°C (depending on how well done you like it). If you don't have a thermometer, take the joint out of the oven and put it on a plate. When you press down on the surface, some of the meat juices will come out. The colour of these juices will tell you whether the meat is cooked:

- ◑ Clear   Well cooked
- ◑ Pink   Rare to medium
- ◑ Red   Undercooked

HOW TO CARVE ●━━▶

WING RIB

Remove the chine bone (broken bone) at the thick end of the joint. Lay the joint fat side uppermost, and cut down in slices, separating the meat from the ribs as you go.

RIB ROAST

Take out the chine bone (use a sharp knife to help) to make it easier to carve. Cut across the joint towards the rib bone in slices, loosening each slice close to the bone.

❧ Lamb ❧

RECOGNISING GOOD LAMB ➟

To check the quality of lamb:

- ◑ the smell shouldn't be strong
- ◑ the lean meat should be a good dull red, and flecked with fat
- ◑ the fat should be a slightly creamy colour, firm and brittle
- ◑ the meat shouldn't be too moist
- ◑ the younger the animal, the more pink and porous the bones. In older animals the bones are whiter, denser and more inclined to splinter
- ◑ the meat should never be slimy, discoloured or smelly

CUTS AND HOW TO COOK THEM ➟

Here's a guide to how best to cook your lamb, depending on the cut.

Cut	Best cooking method
Best end	Roast
Breast	Roast
Chump chop	Grill, fry or braise
Fillet	Grill or fry
Leg	Roast
Loin	Roast
Loin chop	Grill, fry or braise
Middle neck	Stew
Saddle	Roast or pot roast
Scrag end	Stew
Shoulder	Roast

HOW TO TELL WHEN IT'S COOKED •━━▶

If you have a meat thermometer, the temperature should be 60–80°C depending on how well cooked you like it. If you don't have a thermometer, put the joint on a plate and press on it firmly until the meat juices are released. These should be clear or very slightly pink.

HOW TO CARVE •━━▶

It's easy to carve a boned joint, or a best end (which you just slice into cutlets). It's those damn bones you can't actually see inside the leg and shoulder joints that are so tricky. There's no single recommended way to carve a joint, but here are some tips.

LEG

Hold the end of the bone. Now carve into it at an angle of 45° to create a succession of slices. Keep working down the bone, turning it every so often when you feel it will help.

SHOULDER

This is the really tricky one. There's no perfect secret trick I'm afraid, but your best bet is to carve the flesh side of the joint – not the skin side – to get decent sized slices. Once you've done that, at least you can see the bones to carve round them. Good luck.

⊷ *Pork* ⊷

RECOGNISING GOOD PORK ⊷

Pork is a much paler colour than lamb or beef. When choosing a good cut, or assessing the quality of one you've already bought, here's what to look for:

- ◐ the meat should not smell too strong
- ◐ the lean meat should be pale pink and firm
- ◐ the fat should be whiter than that of lamb or beef, and smooth
- ◐ the bones should be pinkish
- ◐ the meat should never be smelly, slimy or discoloured

CUTS AND HOW TO COOK THEM ⊷

Different cooking methods suit different cuts of meat. Here's a quick guide for pork.

Cut	Best cooking method
Belly	Roast or pot roast, or slice and grill, fry or barbecue
Fillet (tenderloin)	Roast, fry or grill
Leg Roast	Roast, or cut into chops and grill or fry
Shoulder	Roast, or cut up to stew
Spare ribs	Grill or barbecue

HOW TO TELL WHEN IT'S COOKED ⊷

If you have a meat thermometer the meat should be 75–85°C. If not, take the meat out of the oven, put it on a plate and press it firmly until the meat juices run out. These should be clear.

♦ *Chef's tip*

To make really crackly crackling, you need to score the rind and then rub in plenty of salt and oil. Start the roast off at a high temperature for the first quarter of an hour, and don't baste it during cooking.

HOW TO CARVE ●━━▶

LEG

It's pretty straightforward carving most pork joints. the tricky one is the leg. So here's the gist. Start crackling side up. Make a series of downward cuts to the bone, keeping them fairly thin. Run the knife underneath the whole section, along the bone,to free the slices. Turn the joint over and carve from this side horizontally, parallel to the bone.

BACON, GAMMON AND HAM ●━━▶

What's the difference? Well, here's the gist:

Bacon	Cured flesh of a pig reared for bacon. It can be either:
	◐ smoked – stronger flavoured and keeps well
	◐ green/unsmoked – milder taste and doesn't store for as long
Gammon	The hind leg of a bacon pig
Ham	Cooked gammon served cold is known as ham, though purists will tell you that technically a ham is removed from the pig before curing

Here's how you can recognise good quality bacon and gammon:

- ⓞ the smell is stronger than with uncured meats but should be pleasant
- ⓞ the lean should be firm and deep pink
- ⓞ the fat should be smooth and white
- ⓞ the rind should be thin and unwrinkled
- ⓞ there should be no sliminess, stickiness or unpleasant smell

For more information on cooking gammon see the Christmas section, pages 146–157.

The main kinds of offal you're likely to want to use are liver, kidneys and heart. I haven't included things like sweetbreads and tongue because you're not likely to be cooking them unless you know what you're doing. I considered including tripe but I couldn't bring myself to write about it as my personal view is that it's so revolting as to be inedible.

LIVER

How you deal with liver depends on the kind of liver you have bought. Tougher liver requires longer, slower cooking. If you're wondering how to cook it, here's a rough guide. (You'll find chicken livers later in the book, under poultry.)

Type of liver	Best cooking method
Calves' liver	Slice and then grill or fry
Lamb's liver	Slice and then grill or fry

Ox liver	Braise or casserole
Pig's liver	Braise or casserole, or use in paté

RECOGNISING GOOD LIVER

- ◗ Liver should look fresh and smooth.
- ◗ It should be moist.
- ◗ It shouldn't contain too many tubes.
- ◗ It should never smell unpleasant.

HOW TO PREPARE LIVER

Start by removing the membrane from the outside, along with any gristle or fat. If there are any large veins running through the flesh, hold the end of the vein with one hand and use a sharp knife to separate the flesh from it. Discard the vein.

KIDNEYS ⚊●

The important thing when cooking kidneys is not to overcook them as they dry out very easily. Here are the best ways to cook different kinds of kidneys.

Type of kidneys	Best cooking method
Calves' kidneys	Grill or fry, or use in casseroles
Lamb's kidneys	Grill or fry, whole or cut up
Ox kidney	Casseroles, puddings and pies (particularly steak and kidney)
Pig's kidney	Grill or fry, or use in casseroles

RECOGNISING GOOD KIDNEYS

- ◗ If the outer suet layer has been removed, make sure the kidneys haven't dried out.
- ◗ Kidneys should never smell unpleasant.

HOW TO PREPARE KIDNEYS

Kidneys have three parts that need to be removed. Firstly there is a layer of white fat or suet around the outside which needs to come off. If you've bought your kidneys at a supermarket this will probably already have been done. Then you need to remove the transparent membrane around the outside that holds the lobes together (this may also have been done). Finally you need to get rid of the fatty core, which is too tough to eat. This is most easily done using a pair of scissors.

> **Rule of thumb**
> *Eat kidneys as fresh as possible. Don't keep them for more than a day or so before using.*

HEART ⚊●

Heart tends to be tough unless you cook is very slowly, so the best cooking method for all varieties is braising. Lamb's hearts, being smaller, are usually cooked whole; other types are generally sliced.

RECOGNISING GOOD HEARTS

(I'm sure there's a joke in there somewhere.)

- ☼ Heart should not be too fatty.
- ☼ It should not have too many tubes.
- ☼ The inside should be moist and not sticky.
- ☼ Heart should never smell unpleasant.

HOW TO PREPARE HEART

All you need to do is to remove the tubes, and take off any excess fat.

Poultry and game

Roasting times and temperatures

Bird	Minutes per lb/400g	Roasting temperature
Chicken	20 minute per lb + 20 minutes	190°C/375°F/gas mark 5/ baking oven
Duck	25 minutes per lb + 20 minutes	180°C/350°F/gas mark 4/ baking oven
Goose	20 minutes per lb + 20 minutes	220°C/425°F/gas mark 7/ roasting oven
Turkey	20 minutes per lb + 20 minutes	180°C/350°F/gas mark 4/ baking oven

Rule of thumb
Allow about an extra 30 minutes cooking time if the bird is stuffed.

How to tell when it's cooked

Pierce the thickest part of the leg. If the juices run clear with no trace of pinkness, the bird is cooked. If you use a meat thermometer it should read at least 70–75°C/

160–170°F. Duck can be served pink, in which case the juices will still have a trace of blood in them, and the meat thermometer should read at least 57°C/135°F.

Chef's tip

You're supposed to rest meat and poultry for about 10 minutes before you carve it. This is because it allows the meat to settle so that carving is easier and you lose less of the juices in the process. The meat will stay hot despite what you might imagine, as it has built up a lot of internal heat during cooking.

Portion sizes

No point buying a small chicken if you've got 10 for lunch. But how many people should you reckon to feed from one bird? Here's a rough guide to calculating portions from the total weight of an unboned bird. Obviously this is for the average appetite – you may need to adjust it to suit your particular guests.

Bird	Allowance per person
Chicken	12oz/300g
Duck	$^{1}/_{2}$ duck
Goose	$1^{1}/_{2}$lbs/700g
Turkey	1lb/400g

Traditional accompaniments

Here's a quick reminder of the traditional accompaniments to roast poultry, along with the gravy.

Bird	Accompaniments
Chicken	Bread sauce, streaky bacon
Duck	Apple sauce
Goose	Apple or gooseberry sauce, sage and onion stuffing
Turkey	Cranberry sauce, bread sauce, stuffing, chipolata sausages

How to stuff a bird for roasting

This is a controversial subject. The health and safety expert say you should never stuff the cavity of a bird as the stuffing may never cook through properly, whereas the traditionalists will tell you that they've always done it without any ill effects. Current recommendations are usually that you should cook the stuffing separately in the same oven as the bird, to reduce the risk of food poisoning.

There is another option, which is gaining popularity, and that is that you put the stuffing under the skin instead of in the cavity. As well as avoiding the health issue, this has other benefits too:

◐ Since the heat reaches it sooner than in the cavity, it has more opportunity to give flavour to the meat.
◐ It protects the breast meat.
◐ Any fat it contains will in effect baste the meat and help to keep it moist as it cooks.

If you're now convinced to give it a try, here's how to do it. Lift the skin at the neck end, around the wishbone, and draw it carefully back, without breaking it, until you've exposed as much of the breast as you need. Push the stuffing in between the skin and the breast, distributed as evenly as you can muster. Then pull the skin back into place over the stuffing and tuck it back under the bird.

Turkey and goose

These birds are most commonly cooked at Christmas, so I've included them in the Christmas section. See pages 146–157. Cuts of turkey can be treated similarly to cuts of chicken (below).

Chicken

RECOGNISING GOOD CHICKEN

- The breast should be plump and firm.
- The breast bone should be supple.
- The skin should be white and unbroken.
- There should be no stickiness.
- Chicken should never smell unpleasant.

Corn fed chicken look quite yellowish, while broiler fowl may have a faint bluish tint. Free range chickens are more strongly coloured and the flesh is slightly firmer.

HOW TO JOINT A CHICKEN

It sometimes happens that you find yourself with a whole chicken and want to separate it out into pieces. This is certainly the most economical way to prepare chicken, so long as you can use all the meat. The process is similar to carving, but with two main differences: firstly, the meat, and especially the joints, are much harder to get through when the chicken is raw. And secondly, you can hold the chicken easily because it's cold. So here's the basic method:

1 Point the legs towards you, breastbone uppermost.
2 Pull one of the legs out from the body and cut through the skin to expose the area where the thigh meets the body.
3 Work a knife between the ball and socket joint to cut the thigh away from the body. The trick is to find the weaker point where you can cut through cartilage and tendons rather than through bone. Repeat this with the other leg.
4 If you want to divide the leg into thigh and drumstick, pull open the joint in the middle of it and, using a similar process, find the joint and separate the two parts of the leg. If the feet are still attached to the drumstick, remove these at the first joint.
5 The wings are attached in a broadly similar fashion to the legs, so use the same technique to separate these from the body.
6 Now remove the wishbone, using the knife to free it.
7 Run the knife between the flesh of the breast and the ribs/breastbone while easing the flesh away, to separate the flesh in two sections, one on each side of the breastbone.

CUTS AND HOW TO COOK THEM ●━━◆

Broadly speaking, apart from specific recipes which may call for a particular part of the chicken, you can use all the main cuts for any purpose, all being equally tender.

However, the presence of bones or skin make some cuts more readily or traditionally used for certain purposes. So here's a quick guide to how best to use that packet of chicken pieces in the fridge that needs eating.

Cut	Best cooking method
Breast	Fry, grill or casserole
Drumstick	Roast or casserole
Thigh	Roast or casserole
Wing	Deep fry, grill or roast
Carcass	Boil up with vegetables to make stock or soup

CHICKEN LIVERS

These are naturally very tender and flavoursome. To prepare chicken livers you simply need to cut or scrape away any green patches, membrane, and fibrous parts at the centre of each.

Chicken livers are best either cooked and blended into patés or terrines, or cooked quickly and served warm – most commonly in salads, risottos and pasta sauces. If you fry them, a couple of minutes in very hot oil should be plenty – the danger is that you will overcook them and make them tough. They should be served still pink in the middle.

HOW TO CARVE A ROAST CHICKEN ━━▶

After resting the bird for a few minutes, place it breast side up on the carving dish (or whatever you want to carve it on).

◐ First remove the leg on one side, and separate the

drumstick and thigh if the chicken is large. Then
remove the wing on that side.
- Now do the same on the other side.
- Now slice the white meat off the breast one side at a
time.

✦— *Duck* —✦

There are four main types of duck you're likely to be able
to buy. Here's a rough guide to the difference:
Aylesbury Classic English duck bred for eating. Barbary
(or Muscovy): a French duck with darker meat than
Aylesbury duck. Gressingham from Suffolk: a cross
between Aylesbury, Barbary and wild duck. It has less fat
than other farmed breeds. Wild duck: the least fatty, and
can be tougher so needs to be well cooked and served in
slices rather than chunks. Generally smaller than farmed
duck.Usually Mallard (though it doesn't have to be)
which is in season from September until April.

RECOGNISING GOOD DUCK ✦—▶

- The breast should be plump.
- The lower back should be pliable.
- There should be no stickiness.
- Duck should never smell unpleasant.

HOW TO JOINT A DUCK ✦—▶

The method here is essentially the same as for chicken
(see page 27), though it's less common to separate the leg
into two pieces.

CUTS AND HOW TO COOK THEM —●

Apart from whole duck, the only cuts you're likely to be dealing with are breasts or whole legs. Duck is rather too fatty to casserole or stew (though it's perfectly possible of course).

Cut	Best cooking method
Breast	Fry, grill or roast
Leg	Deep fry, grill or roast

DUCK LIVERS

As for chicken livers (see page 29).

HOW TO CARVE A ROAST DUCK —●

If you don't happen to own a set of poultry shears, carve duck in the same way as chicken (see page 29).

If you do happen to have some poultry shears kicking around:

- ◐ cut along the breastbone from one end of the bird to the other
- ◐ open up the duck and cut along either side of the backbone until the duck is in two halves
- ◐ put half the duck on a board and use a carving knife to cut between the wing and the leg so it forms two portions
- ◐ repeat with the other half

⚬— *Game* —⚬

WHEN IS IT IN SEASON? ⚬—▶

You can buy most game nowadays, via good mail order companies if not from your local butcher. However, there's no point deciding you fancy cooking fresh pheasant in June – you won't be able to get hold of it. Generally speaking there's no game in season in May, June and July, but all game have their own season. Here's a rough guide to what you can find when:

January	Duck, guinea fowl, hare, partridge, pheasant, pigeon, rabbit
February	Duck, guinea fowl, hare, pigeon, rabbit
March	Duck, hare, pigeon, rabbit
April	Duck, hare, pigeon, rabbit
May	
June	
July	
August	Grouse (from the glorious 12th)
September	Duck, grouse, guinea fowl, partridge, pigeon, venison
October	Duck, grouse, guinea fowl, hare, partridge, pheasant
November	Duck, grouse, guinea fowl, hare, partridge, pheasant, rabbit
December	Duck, grouse, guinea fowl, hare, partridge, pheasant, rabbit

RECOGNISING GOOD GAME ———●

- Birds, hares and rabbits should be in good condition and not wet, bruised or damaged by shot.
- Birds should be plump for their size.
- Plumage or fur should be in good condition.
- A strong smell needn't put you off.

HOW TO COOK GAME ———●

You won't often be cooking game unless you're an expert anyway. But maybe your neighbour has given you a brace of pheasant, or you fancied the look of those guinea fowl in the supermarket. So here are a few pointers when choosing, preparing or cooking game.

GROUSE

Grouse is usually hung for long enough to give it a strong gamey taste. Generally speaking a grouse will serve only one person.

Roasting time: approximately 40 minutes at 180°C/350°F/ gas mark 4/baking oven bottom

GUINEA FOWL

This is quite mild tasting for game. It has a tendency to dry out so either casserole or braise it, or keep it well basted if roasting.

Roasting time: 20 minutes per lb/400g at 200°C/400°F/ gas mark 6/baking oven top

Chef's tip

In the unlikely event that you find yourself having to pluck a bird for the first time, here are some tips. Cut the

skin along the length of the bird and remove it, feathers and all. This of course is only useful if you don't need the skin. If you do need the skin and have to pluck it:

- ◑ *wet your hands*
- ◑ *pluck away from you, pulling the feathers in the direction they grow*
- ◑ *Pluck from the breast towards the neck*

PARTRIDGE

Often considered to be tastier than pheasant, partridge are also smaller and only really serve one person each.

Roasting time: 25 minutes per lb/400g at 200°C/400°F/ gas mark 6/baking oven top

PHEASANT

This generally feeds between two and four people. Young pheasant can be roasted but older (more flavoursome) birds are tougher, so it's better to braise or casserole them.

Roasting time: 25 minutes per lb/400g at 200°C/400°F/ gas mark 6/baking oven top

PIGEON

Pigeon meat is dark and tasty. Allow one bird per person.

Roasting time: 15–20 minutes on each side at 200°C/ 400°F/ gas mark 6/baking oven top

Rule of thumb

Smaller, younger game birds are generally suitable for roasting, while older and larger ones will be better braised or casseroled. The smallest game birds can even be grilled.

QUAIL

It's easiest to eat quail with your fingers (the bones can be quite fiddly and irritating). Allow one per person, though sometimes two seems more hospitable if they're very small.

Roasting time: 20–25 minutes per lb/400g at 200°C/ 400°F/ gas mark 6/baking oven top

RABBIT AND HARE

Farmed rabbit has pale, mild tasting flesh, while wild rabbit is dark and gamey. Hare is darker and stronger flavoured than rabbit. It is quite dry so it's often marinated before cooking, or casseroled.

HOW TO CARVE A GAME BIRD ⚬━●

Unless you're roasting a small bird to serve whole, you need to carve game birds as for duck (see page 31).

Fish and seafood

— Buying fish —

RECOGNISING GOOD FISH

There are few things more revolting than fish that has gone off, quite apart from the likelihood of food poisoning, and the smell is often the best giveaway that fish or shellfish are past their best. Apart from the smell, however, here are a few more indicators to help you make sure that the fish you're buying is good – or the fish in your fridge is still OK to eat.

WHOLE FISH

- The eyes should be clear, bright and bulging slightly.
- The gills should be bright red or pinky red.
- The scales should be close-set, flat, shiny and with none missing.
- The skin should be shiny and moist, never gritty.
- The flesh should be firm and moist.
- The fish should feel stiff rather than limp.
- The eyes, gills and flesh should not be slimy.

PREPARED FISH

- The flesh should be firm and moist.
- It should be translucent rather than milky, without discolouration.

SMOKED FISH

- The flesh should be dry and firm.
- The skin should be glossy.
- The smell should be nice and smoky.

SHELLFISH

- *Molluscs* such as mussels and oysters should be alive (and you should cook them the same day). The shells should be whole, uncracked and slightly open. Tap them sharply and make sure they close in response. If they don't, the mollusc may be dead and unfit to eat.
- *Shrimps* and *prawns* should be dry, firm, and bright rather than dull looking.
- *Crabs* should have all their legs intact. The shell should be rough and feel heavy.
- *Lobsters* should have all their legs intact. The shell should be clean, the tail slightly springy, and they should feel heavy for their size.

Rule of thumb
Fish goes off faster than meat or poultry, and should be eaten as fresh as possible, preferably within 24 hours of buying it.

CONSERVING FISH STOCKS ●——▶

The Marine Conservation Society are very concerned that overfishing is threatening some species of fish, and some marine habitats. They urge the rest of us to help by avoiding buying those fish that are most at risk, and opting instead for those that are most responsibly fished or farmed. The following lists show the most commonly

available fish that are currently at the top and bottom of
the league table: those we should most avoid and those
we can eat without eco-guilt. So if marine conservation is
something you feel strongly about, this guide should help.
Any fish that appear on neither list come somewhere in the
middle; they are not at high risk but there is some concern.

Fish you can eat without guilt	Fish to avoid
Clam (if sustainably harvested)	Atlantic cod (from over-fished stocks)
Coley (from North Sea and West of Scotland	Atlantic halibut
Dover sole (from Eastern channel)	Atlantic salmon (wild)
Herring (from most sources)	European hake
Hoki	Grey mullet
Lemon sole (not beam-trawl caught)	Haddock (from overfished stocks)
Mackerel (line caught from Cornwall)	Monkfish
Mussels (if sustainably harvested)	Orange roughy
Oysters (farmed)	Plaice (from overfished stocks)
Pacific cod (line caught)	Seabass (trawl caught)
Pacific haddock (line caught)	Shark

Pacific salmon (from Alaska)	Skates and rays
Red mullet (not from Mediterranean)	Swordfish
Salmon (farmed)	Tiger prawns (unless organically farmed)
Whiting (from English Channel)	Tuna (unless dolphin friendly) Turbot (from North Sea)

It is now mandatory to label fish with information about where they were caught. Many fish are considered fine to eat so long as you make sure they are from the right source. For the full lists, more information or up-to-date lists if you're reading an old copy of this book, you can visit **www.fishonline.org**.

How to prepare fish

Broadly speaking, fish divide into two categories for preparing: round fish and flat fish (when it comes to cooking they're often divided into two other categories: white fish and oily fish).

If you're not used to preparing fish it can be rather daunting, but in fact it's easier than it looks. The worst you can do is make a bit of a mess of it.

ROUND FISH

CLEANING AND GUTTING

❍ To gut a round fish, start by slitting right along its

underside from tail to head. Then you simply pull out all the guts. Hold the cavity open under running cold water to clean it out thoroughly.

○ You can remove the scales by scraping them off with the blunt side of a knife (unless you happen to own a fish scaler, in which case now is your chance to use it). Scrape towards the head. If you're not planning to eat the skin you don't need to scale it.

○ If you don't want to leave the head on you can simply cut it off with a sharp knife.

FILLETING

○ If you want to fillet the fish, cut the flesh along the length of the backbone, keeping the knife just above it (it doesn't matter which way up it is because you're about to turn it over and repeat this on the other side). Now run the knife between the flesh and the bones, starting at the head end, to separate them. You should end up with a fillet. Repeat this on the other side of the fish.

○ To skin a fillet, put it skin side down on a board. Hold the tail end and cut the flesh at angle with a sharp knife, as close to the tail as you can, until it meets the skin. Then angle the knife to cut between the flesh and the skin. Hold the tail tightly and pull it towards you so it pulls the fillet up past the knife, separating the flesh from the skin.

FLAT FISH ●━━▶

CLEANING AND GUTTING

○ Make a cut along the underside of the fish (which, being a flat fish, looks more like one edge of it). This

will open up the stomach so you can remove the guts.
- ○ Trim off the fins and gills with scissors.
- ○ If you plan to eat the white skin, scale it with the back of a knife working towards the head. The dark skin is generally not eaten, so no point scaling it.
- ○ If you don't want to cook the head, now's a good time to cut it off.
- ○ Rinse the fish under cold running water to clean it well.
- ○ If you're going to fillet the fish in a minute, leave the skin on (except that, for some reason, the dark skin of Dover sole is usually removed before filleting).
- ○ If you're planning to cook the fish whole it's customary to remove the dark skin only. Put the fish white side up. Make a small cut near the tail to separate the skin from the flesh, keeping the knife in the incision. Keeping the blade flate between the skin and the flesh, grab the tail end of the skin firmly and pull it. This should pull the skin and flesh past the knife to separate them.

FILLETING

- ○ To fillet the fish into two fillets, cut right round the edge of the fish on the top side, turning it round as you go to get a good angle. Now repeat this process but cutting futher towards the backbone, separating the flesh from the bone in long smooth strokes of the knife. This should free up the whole top fillet, which you can carefully lift away. Repeat on the other side.
- ○ To fillet the fish into four (which you'd probably be doing because it's a large fish) cut down through the flesh above the backbone until the knife meets the spine. Working from the backbone to the edge of the fish, hold the blade flat against the bone and use long

smooth strokes of the knife to separate the flesh from the bones. Now remove the other fillet on the same side, before turning the fish over and repeating.

Chef's tip

Notoriously slippery things, fish. If you can't get a firm grip on the skin or tail when you need to, hold it in a towel.

— *How to prepare other seafood* —

If you're not used to cooking seafood it can seem like quite a scary prospect. But most things aren't as scary as they first look, and lobster, mussels, squid and the rest of them are perfectly easy to prepare if you know how. So here's how.

CRAB ——▶

If you want to cook crab from raw you should buy it alive. The recommended way to kill and cook a live crab is to plunge it into salted water, bring it back to the boil and continue to boil it. This will take between 10 and 25 minutes depending on the size of the crab. There is another way of killing it involving a sharp knife but I don't want to write about it.

If you buy your crab ready cooked, make sure it has all its legs and both claws intact. It should smell pleasant in a salty kind of way, and the shell should be a fresh orange colour.

To prepare the crab once cooked:

- remove the legs and claws by twisting them, and set them on one side. Remove the tail flap, or apron, from the underside
- crack the central section of the soft undershell so you can prise it off – the main body of the crab should come with it
- there are now certain parts you need to remove: the stomach sac just behind the mouth and the gills (charmingly known as dead men's fingers). These should be obvious – they're not poisonous, merely unpleasant
- now you can cut or crack the main body section into pieces so you can dig out the white flesh and set it on one side
- next, spoon out and save the dark meat that is in the shell, and any roe
- using whatever tools you can lay your hands on – nut-crackers, a small hammer, knife etc – open up and extract the meat from the legs and claws (or you can serve the claws whole)
- if you want to you can replace the meat attractively inside the shell before servng it

LOBSTER

If you buy your lobster live you can kill and cook it by plunging it into boiling water, bringing it back to the boil and then cooking it for a further 15–20 minutes. If you want to split it and grill it before serving, only $^1/_2$ cook it at this stage.

- A lobster has a central line conveniently marked on its underbelly. If you simply want to split it before grilling you can now cut along the central line and open it up.

◐ If you want to extract the flesh, don't do this yet. First, twist off the legs and claws. You can now extract the flesh using nutcrackers or a hammer to break them open if necessary.

◐ Hold the tail section in one hand and the body/head in the other. Twist and pull the tail section to separate it. Turn the tail upside down and cut along the centre of the underside. Prize the two sides open and remove the flesh. On a good day it should come out in one piece.

◐ You still have the main body section to deal with. Cut along the dotted line (OK it's not really dotted) down the centre of the underbelly with a sharp knife or scissors, and remove the flesh.

◐ You want to discard: the pale grey intestine that runs the length of the body, the grey gills near the head, and the gritty stomach sac near the head.

◐ You may want to keep: the red coral (roe), the greenish-grey liver near the head.

Chef's tip

If you put a live lobster in the freezer for 10 minutes before killing it, it will fall asleep. This may make you feel better.

MUSSELS, CLAMS AND COCKLES ◦━━◀

Mussels are best bought live. They are rarely served raw, while clams and cockles can be cooked like mussels or served raw like oysters.

- Put them in a bowl of cold water and pick over them. Scrape off any barnacles with a knife, and scrub the shells to get rid of any grit and sand.
- There is usually a stringy 'beard' on the outside of the shell; pull this off and discard it.
- Remove any molluscs that don't close when you tap them sharply.
- After cooking (usually by steaming) remove any that haven't opened up, along with any that smell suspicious.

OYSTERS

Get rid of any oysters with shells that are partly open, or those that smell fishy, as they are probably dead and could give you food poisoning. Try to keep the oyster flat as you open it so you don't spill the brine inside it. Hold the oyster with a towel to protect your fingers from the sharp shell.

- If you're planning to serve the oysters raw on the shell, scrub them thoroughly before opening.
- Use a strong knife with a flat blade if you don't have an oyster knife. Hold the oyster flat and insert the knife into the hinge. Twist it to open up the oyster.
- Run the knife between the oyster and the top shell to separate them. Remove the top shell.
- Without spilling the liquid, slide the knife between the oyster and the bottom shell to separate them.

SCALLOPS

You're unlikely to buy scallops unopened, but just in case you do: run a thin, sharp, flexible knife between the top and bottom shells to separate them. Don't push the blade in too far or you may damage the scallop meat.

- Separate the meat from the top shell carefully with a knife, and discard the top shell.
- Slide the knife gently under the meat to separate it from the bottom shell.
- Use your fingers to separate the various parts of the scallop. You want the firm white lump of flesh, and the pink coral (roe). Get rid of everything else (the grey viscera and membrane).
- When eaten raw, scallops are usually served in the more rounded of the two shells.

SHRIMPS AND PRAWNS

If you've bought raw prawns, simmer them in water to 3–5 minutes to cook them. Allow 8–10 minutes for Dublin Bay prawns or langoustines.

- Once the prawn is cooked, snap the head and then pull it off and discard it. Snap the tail and pull it off gently leaving the flesh behind.
- Peel off the shell and legs using your fingers.
- Alternatively prepare them raw and then cook them in, say, a stir-fry.

SQUID

A squid comes in two main sections: the body, known as the mantle, and the tentacles. The inedible parts are the eye, the beak (mouth) and the quill (a flexible flat bone-like structure inside the mantle). There is also a small black sac which contains the ink, which you can use to colour sauces and pasta. For this reason it pays to pre-pare squid over a bowl of some kind.

○ You should be able to pull the mantle and the tentacles apart into two sections easily. The head, eye and ink sac will come with the tentacles.

○ Pull the quill out of the mantle and throw it away, and cut off the 'wings' on either side of the mantle.

○ If the squid is large enough to warrant it you can skin the mantle – the skin should come away easily.

○ Cut the tentacles from the head just above the eye. The tentacles should still be joined at the top. Keep the ink sac if you want to use it. If you open up the tentacles you'll find the beak. Pull this out and throw it away.

○ You can now either cut the squid up or leave it whole, depending on the recipe.

Cooking fish

You can cook most fish in most ways: fry, grill, bake, steam or poach. Here are a few pointers for whichever method you choose. You should always do your best not to overcook fish as this damages the texture. It is the thickness of the fish that determines how long it will take to cook.

Rule of thumb
Most fish can be cooked by most methods. However oily fish don't poach or steam well.

BAKING

You can bake fish in parcels of foil or greaseproof paper to prevent it drying out. This also means you can add butter, lemon juice and herbs to add moisture and flavour. Suitable fish for baking whole include: bream, hake, mackerel, salmon, sea bass and trout. You can bake steaks or fillets of such fish as cod, hake, halibut, mackerel, plaice (skinned), salmon and sole.

Bake fish at around 190°C/375°F/gas mark 5/baking oven middle:

Fish	Approximate baking time
Whole	10 minutes per inch (2.5cm) of thickness
Steaks	10 minutes per inch (2.5cm) of thickness
Fillets	6 minutes per 1/2 inch (1.25cm) of thickness

FRYING ●——◗

Before you fry fish – deep or shallow – you need to coat it in egg and then flour, batter or breadcrumbs, to protect it. Frying is generally used for fillets or small fish such as whitebait.

SHALLOW FRYING

Aim to turn delicate fish just once half way through the frying process to avoid damaging it.

DEEP FRYING

The key to any kind of frying is to make sure the oil is hot enough before you put the fish in, otherwise the coating won't seal properly. If you have an oil thermometer for deep frying, aim for at least 180°C before you start to cook the fish.

Rule of thumb
When deep frying fish, allow about 8 minutes for every 1 inch of thickness.

GRILLING

This works for most fish, and is especially good for whole oily fish such as mackerel and trout. It's best to grill at a moderate rather than high heat, and score the flesh of fish that is on the bone to encourage the heat to spread evenly. Oily fish is naturally moist, but white fish is best brushed with melted butter to prevent it drying out. Turn the fish half way through cooking unless you have very thin fillets.

Thickness of fish	Approximate grilling time	Distance from grill
1 inch/2.5cm	4 minutes each side	4–6 inches/10–15cm
$^1/_2$ inch/1.25cm	2 minutes each side	2 inches/5cm

BARBECUING

Plenty of fish and shellfish barbecue beautifully, including haddock, prawns, salmon, sardines, scallops, sea bass, trout and tuna. It's the best way to cook kippers if you want to keep the smell out of the kitchen. You can either use a griddle pan, a barbecue fish basket, or cook them straight on the rack. Scallops, prawns or small pieces of fish can be cooked as kebabs.

Leave the skin on whole fish when you barbecue it as this will help keep the fish in one piece. You only need scale it if you're going to eat the skin. If the rack is clean and hot when you put the fish on, it's less likely to stick to it.

Cooking times are very roughly the same as for grilling; the recommendation is that fish steaks and fillets should be at least $1/2$ inch (1.25cm) thick to prevent them over-cooking.

POACHING •——●

You can cook fish gently in flavoured liquid, which is often then used in any accompanying sauce. Typical flavours are herbs, onions, lemon or wine. One of the great advantages of poaching is that it keeps the fish moist.

Classic fish for poaching include halibut, salmon, sea bass, skate wings and whole trout. As a general guide, poach fish for approximately 6 minutes for each inch (2.5cm) of thickness.

STEAMING •——●

Steaming uses only a small amount of water but still keeps the fish moist. If you don't have a purpose-made steamer you can put the fish on a buttered, heatproof plate that sits over a pan of boiling water. It's important that the fish neither touches the boiling water nor boils dry, although you can put shellfish right in the pan with the liquid. Steaming is a great cooking method for lots of fish, including flatfish, John Dory and sea bass, as well as clams and mussels.

Allow approximately 8 minutes for each 1 inch/2.5cm of thickness.

Chef's tip

Many people now feel that to prevent overfishing of cod they prefer to buy other varieties of fish. If you want to substitute cod in any recipe you can use haddock instead.

TRADITIONAL ACCOMPANIMENTS

Certain flavours go very well with fish, and are classically served along side them. Many of these can accompany just about any kind of fish cooked in a particular way. For example:

Cooking method	Accompaniment
Baked fish	Herb or anchovy butter, sauces (eg white wine, tomato, mushroom)
Deep fried fish	Tartare sauce, lemon wedges
Grilled fish	Herb butter
Poached fish	Herb or anchovy butter, Hollandaise sauce, mushroom sauce
Poached fish served cold	Slices of cucumber

Herb butter, by the way, is any butter than has been softened and mixed with finely chopped herbs and then rehardened in the fridge. Examples include parsley, mixed herb, chive, dill or tarragon butters, or you can use non-herb butters such as anchovy, lemon or garlic.

In addition to these general accompaniments, certain

seafood has its own traditional accompaniment. Here are some of the most popularly used ones.

Cod	Parsley sauce, Mornay (cheese) sauce
Herring	Mustard sauce
Mackerel	Gooseberry sauce, rhubarb sauce
Mussels	White wine sauce
Oysters	Lemon juice, tabasco, pint of Guinness
Salmon (poached or baked)	Hollandaise sauce
Salmon (smoked)	Brown bread and butter, lemon wedges
Skate	Black butter

Vegetables, fruit and nuts

WHAT IS IT?

There's a lot of controversy about whether rhubarb should be categorised as a fruit (because you generally eat it sweetened) or a vegetable (because you eat the stem). You can't please all of the people all of the time, so I'm just putting it under fruit. Similarly I'm calling a tomato a vegetable. Please don't write in.

Vegetables

WHEN IS IT IN SEASON?

Not only is it hard to find some vegetables when they're out of season, but they won't be very tasty even if you can find them. So if you're planning a meal, here's a quick guide to what vegetables are in season when in the UK. Of course, imported vegetables are often available outside these times.

I should just point out that this isn't an exact science. You may get very early or late varieties of a different vegetable outside the months indicated, the weather varies from year to year, and you can debate endlessly whether something grown in a polytunnel really counts or not. But this is a good rough guide.

January	Beetroot, cabbage (all types), carrots, cauliflower, celeriac, celery, chard, Jerusalem artichokes, kohlrabi, leeks, parsnips, shallots, spinach, sprouts, swede
February	Beetroot, broccoli, cabbage (all types), carrots, cauliflower, celeriac, celery, leeks, parsnips, salsify, shallots, spinach, sprouts, swede, turnips
March	Beetroot, broccoli, cabbage, calabrese, carrots, cauliflower, celery, leeks, parsnips, spinach, spring greens, spring onions, swede, turnips
April	Broccoli, carrots, leeks, early lettuce and salad leaves, early new potatoes, spring cabbage, spring onions
May	Asparagus, broad beans, cabbage, carrots, cauliflower, lettuce, new potatoes, radishes, salad leaves, spinach
June	Artichokes, asparagus, cabbage, carrots, courgettes, fennel, globe artichokes, green beans, lettuce, mange-tout peas, new potatoes, radishes, salad leaves, tomatoes, watercress
July	Artichokes, asparagus, broad beans, cabbage (spring and summer), carrots, cauliflower, courgettes, cucumber, fennel, French beans, garlic, green beans, lettuce, new potatoes, peas, peppers, radishes, salad leaves, watercress

August	Aubergine, beetroot, cabbage, chard, courgettes, fennel, French beans, leeks, lettuce, marrow, new potatoes, peas, peppers, radishes, runner beans, salad leaves, sweetcorn, tomatoes
September	Aubergine, beetroot, broccoli, cabbage (all varieties), cauliflower, carrots, courgettes, cucumber, curly kale, French beans, leeks, lettuce, marrow, peppers, radishes, red onions, salad leaves, sprouts, swede, sweetcorn, tomatoes, wild mushrooms
October	Beetroot, broccoli, autumn cabbage, carrots, cauliflower, Jerusalem artichokes, leeks, marrow, maincrop potatoes, pumpkin, sprouts, squash, sweetcorn, turnips, wild mushrooms
November	Beetroot, cabbage (red and savoy), carrots, cauliflower, celeriac, celery, Jerusalem artichokes, leeks, parsnips, pumpkin, sprouts, swede
December	Beetroot, cabbage (red), carrots, chard, curly kale, Jerusalem artichokes, leeks, garlic, parsnip, pumpkin, swede, spinach, sprouts, turnip

Broadly speaking vegetables such as potatoes, carrots, onions and some kinds of celery are available all year round, as there are varieties for many times of year and they store well to cover the remaining few months.

HOW MUCH TO COOK

What constitutes an average portion of vegetables? As a rough guide allow 3–4oz (75–100g) per serving, depending on how hungry you think your guests are. That's as an accompaniment, of course. If you're serving the vegetable as the main dish you should allow more. This equates to about 3–4 tablespoons of things like beans, sliced carrots, shredded cabbage or peas. It's about one light-bulb sized potato.

HOW TO PREPARE AND COOK VEGETABLES

You probably know how to peel a potato or remove the outer leaves from a cabbage. But do you know the best way to peel salsify, or which bits of kohlrabi to use? Here's a potted guide to the vegetables you may need advice on dealing with. I'm going to assume you know how to deal with the basics such as carrots or celery.

◐ ***Artichoke, globe*** Cut off the stalk and tough outer leaves, and trim off the top inch or so. Prize the leaves apart and scoop out the prickly 'choke' from the centre. Boil or steam the remaining head. Once cooked, each leaf should be peeled off and the fleshy part at the bottom eaten (dip it in vinaigrette or Hollandaise). The rest of the leaf is discarded. Alternatively, pull off all the leaves and then trim off the stem and leaf bases. You'll need to cut off the central soft cone of leaves left in the middle. Right in the centre is the hairy choke, which you should scoop out with a small spoon, making sure you remove all the fibrous hairs. The remaining bowl shaped artichoke bottom is now ready to cut up and cook.

○ **Artichoke, Jerusalem** Scrub them, and peel them if you have the energy, or just cook them in their skins. If you peel or cut them put them straight into cold water or they'll discolour. Then cook as for any root vegetables and serve as an accompaniment or in stews. They make wonderful soup.

Chef's tip

Be warned that Jerusalem artichokes cause significant flatulence in some people, so maybe think twice before serving them when you have prudish guests for dinner.

○ **Asparagus** Trim off the woody ends of the stems. Sometimes there will be very little to trim, but if they seem tough you may need to take off quite a lot. As a general guide, the point where the stem snaps naturally is the dividing line between the edible and the tough parts. Also trim off any overlarge, tough looking scales. Boil or steam them. If you want to serve them cold, plunge them into cold water as soon as they're cooked to keep their colour.

○ **Aubergine** Remove the stem. You're now supposed to salt, rinse and drain them, according to many recipes, in order to get rid of any bitterness. However this really isn't necessary (as explained delightfully by Nicholas Clee in his book *Don't Sweat the Aubergine*). Aubergines just aren't that bitter. You can now slice, cube or cook them whole, according to the recipe. They will take up a good deal of oil – the best way to cook them as an accompaniment is sliced or cubed in the oven, drizzled with plenty of olive oil, for about half an hour.

Chef's tip

Any vegetable or fruit which discolours once it is peeled can be kept underwater, or tossed in lemon juice.

- **Beansprouts** These need no preparation. Just toss them into salads or stir-frys.
- **Beetroot** Fresh beetroot should be scrubbed clean and then cooked in their skins. You can boil or bake them whole. Peel them after cooking (the skin won't harm you but it's rather tough) or you'll lose some of the colour. Whatever you do you're bound to lose some of the colour eventually into your chopping board, clothing, kitchen cloths – be careful as it gets every-where and stains. You can cook and eat the leaves much as you would spinach (unless you're one of those people who would never cook or eat spinach).
- **Brussels sprouts** may need a reminder of how to cook them. As with a cabbage, peel of the outer leaves and trim the stem. Then make a deep cross in the base of the stem so the heat can penetrate and the sprouts will cook quicker.
- **Celeriac** One of my very favourites. Only the root is eaten; avoid the biggest as these can be woody. Peel it and then either grate it raw into salads or cook as for any root vegetable – boil, steam or braise, or add to soups and stews.
- **Chicory** Remove the base of the stems, and then eat raw in salads (it's quite bitter) or cook as for other leaf vegetables.
- **Chillis** It's the seeds that are really hot, so if you don't like them too hot remove the seeds and cook only the flesh. You may want to wear surgical gloves for very

hot chillis, or at least wash your hands very thoroughly afterwards.

Rule of thumb
This isn't totally infallible but as a fairly reliable guide: the smaller the chilli, the more of a punch it packs.

- **Chinese Cabbage** Milder tasting than most cabbage. Treat this just as you would a white cabbage.
- **Fennel** Remove the leaves, leaving any undamaged stalks. Trim the end off the bulb. You can now slice it in half or more to cook it, or slice thinly into salads. It is most often braised or steamed.
- **Garlic** You buy garlic as a *bulb* which is made up of individual *cloves*. You need to peel the papery skin off the outside of the bulb to get at the cloves, and each clove also needs peeling.
- **Kohlrabi** This is actually a swollen stem and not a root. Treat it as you would a turnip (even if, like me, you would never knowingly eat turnip). Cut off the stems and trim the base. Peel it and use it in stews and soups, or grate it raw into salads.
- **Okra** Simply wash these and trim off the stem. Cook them whole in stews and stir-frys.
- **Pumpkin** This is a bit like a melon with a harder skin. Peel it and remove the seeds, then cut the flesh into chunks for stews, soups and pumpkin pie. You can also cut pumpkin in half, deseed it and then roast it in its skin. Stuff it or put butter and black pepper in the centre.
- **Salsify** This long thin root vegetable should be treated like a parsnip or any other root. Clean thoroughly or

peel thinly, and remove the sprouting top. It is delicious in soups and stews, or in a casserole.

Chef's tip

Just one thing you should know about salsify: it is incredibly sticky to peel so you might find it easier to do underwater.

- **Sorrel** Treat it exactly as you would spinach.
- **Squash** There's a huge variety of squashes available, which divide into hard skinned winter squashes, and the soft skinned summer varieties. For winter squashes the general gist is to remove the skin and seeds, and then cut up the flesh for soups and stews. Alternatively cut them in half, remove the seeds and then roast them – either stuffed or with a bit of butter and black pepper in the middle. Soft skinned summer squashes can be boiled, steamed or roasted and eaten whole. They are more like courgettes.
- **Sweet potato** Treat exactly as for ordinary potatoes. They're delicious roasted in their jackets.
- **Swiss chard** Cook as you would spinach, spring greens or any other green leafy vegetable.
- **Yam** Treat as you would potatoes and sweet potatoes.

Rule of thumb

When you boil any vegetable apart from new potatoes:

If it grows above ground, put it into boiling water.

If it grows below ground, put it into cold water and bring it to the boil.

SKINNING TOMATOES AND PEPPERS

Some recipes demand that you skin tomatoes and peppers, and both of these are near impossible to peel with a vegetable peeler. Each has its own technique:

○ **Tomatoes** Make a cross with a sharp knife in the end opposite the stalk. Put the tomato in a pan of boiling water for about 15 seconds and then remove it with a slotted spoon. The corners of the cut skin should be peeling back now and you can just pull the skin carefully off.

○ **Peppers** Put the pepper under a hot grill, turning occasionally until it is charred all over. Alternatively hold it (using a heatproof cooking fork) in a gas cooker flame. Either way, you then put it in a plastic bag, seal the bag and leave it until it has cooled. The skin should come away really easily.

WHICH POTATO FOR WHICH PURPOSE?

You'll never get a really creamy mash, or a crispy roastie from the wrong variety of potato. Potatoes divide into two broad types – waxy and floury. Waxy potatoes hold their shape well, so are good for baking and as new potatoes in salads, for example. Floury potatoes break up readily, which makes them good for mashing. This is why some potatoes are better suited than others to particular purposes.

The waxy/floury thing is a kind of sliding scale from 'very waxy' all the way through to 'very floury', so potatoes bang in the middle are the most adaptable. The most popular of these all round varieties are Desirée and Maris Piper.

Purpose	Good varieties
Baking	Cara, Desirée, Estima, Marfona
Boiling	Charlotte, Maris Peer, Saxon
Chips	King Edward, Maris Piper, Sante
Mashing	Estima, Romano
New potatoes	Jersey Royal, Nicola
Roasting	King Edward, Red Duke of York, Romano

Of course many of the more old fashioned and harder-to-obtain varieties are delicious. If you can get hold of the likes of Pink Fir Apple potatoes for your salads, or Edzell Blue for mashing, these are often far tastier than the mass produced varieties.

For how to salvage lumpy mash, roasties that won't brown, boiled potatoes that break up or dauphinois potatoes that won't cook, see pages 143–144.

Chef's tip

You should always store potatoes somewhere cool, dark and airy (not in a plastic bag) to keep them eatable for as long as possible. Don't keep them in the fridge because this can make them discolour after cooking, and can damage the taste and texture.

COOKING TIMES

It's hard to be spot-on accurate with cooking times because it depends on how hard you boil the thing, or what size chunks you've cut it into. It also depends whether you like your vegetables still firm or soft right through. But here is a good enough guide to how long you can expect your vegetables to take to cook (in minutes). Boiling times start from when the water boils/comes back to the boil.

Vegetable	Boiling	Steaming	Roasting
Asparagus	3–6	3–6	
Beans (French, runner, green)	5	8	
Beetroot (whole)	45	45	45
Broccoli florets	5–8	10–15	
Brussels sprouts	7	10	
Cabbage (sliced)	5	8	
Carrots (sliced) (chunks)	7–8	10	50–6
Cauliflower florets	4–5	10–12	
Celeriac (chunks)	10	10	
Corn–on–the–cob	4	10	25–30
Leeks (in chunks)	7	12	
Mangetout peas	2–3	7–8	
Mushrooms			20
Parsnips (chunks)	10	15	45 (whole)
Peas (fresh)	4–5	8–10	
Potatoes (whole)	20–25	30	90 (jackets)
Potatoes (chunks)	15–20	30	60 (roast)
Spinach	2	4	

Squash (winter, in chunks)	15	25–30	60 (halved)
Swede (chunks)	10–12	15	
Sweet potatoes (chunks)	25–30	40–45	60
Turnips (chunks)	10–12	15	

Rule of thumb
Roast vegetables at around 190°C/375°F/gas mark 5/ range cooker baking oven

Fruit and nuts

WHEN IS IT IN SEASON?

It's no good planning to make a fresh mandarin trifle in June, or a strawberry shortcake in December. Even if you can get hold of the fruit you want, it won't taste half so good when it's not in season. So here's a guide to when most fruits are at their freshest and best in the UK.

January	Apples and pears (stored), forced rhubarb.
February	Apples and pears (stored), forced rhubarb.
March	Apples and pears (stored), rhubarb.
April	Apples and pears (stored), rhubarb.
May	Early cherries, gooseberries and strawberries in late May, rhubarb.
June	Blackcurrants, cherries, gooseberries, strawberries.

July	Black, red and white currants, blueberries, cherries, loganberries, raspberries, strawberries, tayberries.
August	Apricots, black, red and white currants, blueberries, cherries, loganberries, melons, plums, raspberries, strawberries, tayberries.
September	Apples, blackberries, damsons, figs, grapes, greengages, melons, pears, plums, raspberries.
October	Apples, figs, pears.
November	Apples, pears, quince.
December	Apples, pears.

How to prepare fruit

If you've never been sure whether you can eat the seeds of a papaya, or what to do with a dragon fruit, this quick guide should tell you.

- **Blueberry** These need no preparation apart from washing. You can use them whole and raw, or cook them in pies or to make jams.
- **Cape gooseberry** This Chinese lantern-type fruit is covered in papery leaves. Peel these back to reveal the round orange fruit. You can eat this whole, either raw or cooked.
- **Currants** Red, white or black currents are most easily spearated from the stems by pulling them through a fork. The currants should fall into the bowl (yes, you need to do it over a bowl) and you should be left holding the stem. You can use them fresh though the

flavour is very strong and tart. Or stew them and use in summer pudding, jams, ice cream, pies and more.

- **Crab apple** Too sour to eat raw but they make great jellies and jams, having a high pectin content so they set well. They're just small apples, but so fiddly to peel and core that more usually you would remove the stem and blossom, quarter them and then cook them. You can strain out the skin and pips later.

- **Cranberry** Too sharp to eat raw, so cook them whole for jams, muffins and, of course, cranberry sauce at Christmas time.

- **Damson** This is a small variety of plum, so it has a stone in the middle. You can eat all the rest, either raw or cooked.

Chef's tip

Bananas release a chemical that causes other fruit to ripen faster. So store them near underripe fruit to speed up the ripening, but keep them away from fruit that is at risk of becoming overripe before you get round to eating it. To delay peeled bananas going brown, soak them in cold water for 10 minutes before peeling them.

- **Dragon fruit** There's a case for putting on sunglasses before preparing dragon fruit, at least if you had a heavy night last night. The skin is cerise pink with large scales or bracts, and the flesh bright purple or white with black seeds. Don't eat the skin, but scoop out the flesh which has the seeds embedded in it and eat this.

- **Elderberry** Not eaten raw, but separate the fruits from the stem and use it in jams and wines.

● **Fig** You can eat the whole of the fig, though you may prefer to peel it. It can also be poached.

● **Gooseberry** Remove the stems. Dessert gooseberries can be eaten raw. Other gooseberries need to be cooked and sweetened to make them pleasant, so stew them with sugar or honey to taste.

● **Greengage** This is a delicious variety of plum, so you can eat it skin and all apart from the stone in the middle. Like plums, greengages can be eaten raw or cooked.

● **Kiwi fruit** The skin is normally not eaten, but is sometimes left on if the kiwi is sliced. You eat the black seeds which would be impossible to separate fully from the flesh. They can be eaten whole or sliced in fruit salads. The best way to peel a kiwi is to top and tail it, cut through the skin at one point and then slide a teaspoon between the skin and the flesh and use this to peel it.

Chef's tip

The easiest way to eat a whole kiwi fruit is to halve it with a knife and scoop out the flesh with a teaspoon.

● **Kumquat** This is the smallest of citrus fruits and can be eaten whole, peeled or sliced.

● **Lychee** You need to peel off the bizarre knobbly outer casing to get at the flesh. Inside this is a large stone which you need to discard.

● **Mango** Peel off the skin, and then the funstarts. Inside the mango is a very large flattish stone. You have no easy way of knowing which way this is aligned, but you need to cut the flesh away from it. Alternatively cut the flesh off *before* you peel it, score the flesh down to

the skin in cubes, and then turn the skin 'inside out'.
The flesh will come away easily.

O **Medlar** This is one of those strange fruits which needs
to be left to 'blet' or rot after picking before you can eat
it. You can then eat it whole or use it to make jelly.

O **Papaya** Also known as pawpaw (especially in
Mexico, where *papaya* is a very rude word). You cut
this in half, scoop out the black seeds and eat the
orange flesh. In fact the seeds are also edible and
rather peppery – you can use them as a substitute for
capers. Papaya contains an enzyme that helps tenderise
meat so it's often used in some parts of the world in
casseroles and stews to help cook the meat.

Chef's tip

Freeze seedless grapes, or slices of lemon, in the summer
(or should that be in the freezer) to put in cold drinks to
chill them without diluting them.

O **Passion fruit** The dark skin should be wrinkled
when the fruit is ripe. You don't eat the skin, but cut it
in half and scoop out the orange pulp mixed with the
black seeds. All of this is edible.

O **Pomegranate** Don't eat the skin. Cut it open and
you'll find it's divided into sections with bitter tasting
pith. Between the areas of pith you'll find what you're
after: white seeds surrounded by pink pulp. Use these
in salads, ice cream or sauces, or just eat it out of the
skin.

O **Quince** The white flesh is too sour to eat raw. So peel
it and chop it into chunks or slices and stew, poach or
bake it. It can be used in pies, sauce and – most commonly – jelly.

○ *Rhubarb* This is eaten cooked. Don't eat any of the leaves as these are poisonous. It needs sweetening, so stew it with sugar or honey.

○ *Sharon fruit* This is a bit like a large orange tomato. Discard the green sepals around the stalk and eat everything else. You can just bite into it as you would an apple, or slice it into fruit salads and other dishes.

○ *Star fruit* This has a mild taste with a crunchy texture. Trim off the top and bottom, and the outside edge of each rib. Then slice it across to get the star shape and use it raw (you can cook it but it's a bit pointless as it's really valued for its appearance more than its taste).

Chef's tip

Leftover bananas that are going soft and brown (the point where even reasonable people think twice about eating them) can be used in making bread or healthy milkshakes.

NUTS ━━●

(Warning: this section may contain nuts)

Nuts are very versatile and are used in sweet and savoury dishes. The flavours of different nuts are suited to different foods, so here's a quick guide to what kind of food each nut traditionally goes with.

○ *Almonds* These are the most popular nut worldwide, and are traditionally used in sweet dishes especially. Ground almonds are used to make marzipan and as a thickening agent.

○ **Brazils** Mostly used in cakes and desserts. Once shelled, they go rancid quite quickly because they have a high fat content.

○ **Cashews** Most often used in savoury dishes such as curries, nut roasts and stir-frys.

○ **Chestnuts** Associated with Christmas, chestnuts are used in both sweet and savoury dishes. They are eaten cooked. You can buy them dried or peeled, or peel them yourself (see below) which is rather a fag. They are great in soups and stews, and in stuffings. In sweet dishes they are often combined with chocolate. Dried chestnuts should be soaked for $1^1/_2$ to 2 hours.

○ **Coconut** This is used in both sweet and savoury dishes. Coconut milk is often used in curries and other spicy dishes.

○ **Hazelnuts** Also known as cobnuts, these need to be shelled with nutcrackers. They can then be toasted (see below) or eaten as they are. They are used in both sweet and savoury dishes, and go particularly well with chocolate.

○ **Macadamias** These are delicious, though very hard to shell. They taste even better after roasting and are mostly used in sweet dishes, especially combined with toffee flavours or white chocolate.

○ **Peanuts** Apart from peanut butter, these are most often eaten as a snack though they can go very well in salads and stir-frys.

○ **Pecans** Similar to walnuts but sweeter, pecans are usually used in sweet dishes or bread. Traditionally paired with maple syrup.

○ **Pine nuts** or pine kernels. These are a key ingredient of pesto sauce, they are also used in other savoury dishes such as risotto and salads. They go rancid easily so it can be a good idea to store them in the fridge.

◐ **Pistachios** These green-tinged nuts are generally used in sweet dishes such as ice cream and pastries.

◐ **Walnuts** These are often used whole or in halves, particularly in sweet dishes such as cakes. They are often paired with coffee flavours.

HOW TO TOAST NUTS

Toasting nuts brings out the flavour and is commonly done with flaked almonds, hazelnuts and macadamias especially. Spread them on a baking sheet and put them in an oven at about 180°C/350°F/gas mark 4/range cooker baking oven. Leave them for around 5–8 minutes, or until they are golden.

HOW TO PEEL CHESTNUTS

You can't just crack open a chestnut with nutcrackers as you can with most nuts. If you want to peel them you should either grill, deep fry or boil them to open up the skins and make them easier to peel. Either way you need first to pierce the top of each nut with a sharp knife to prevent it bursting when it gets hot. Then you have three options:

1 Grill them under a hot grill for about three minutes until the skins split.
2 Deep fry them for about three minutes until they start to open.
3 Put them in cold water and bring them to the boil to open the skins.

Whichever you do, you should wait for them to cool down (obviously) and then remove both the shell and the bitter inner skin. Or buy them ready peeled (gets my vote).

Pasta, pulses, rice and grains

— *Pasta* —

I shan't deal with fresh pasta here, on the grounds that if you can make your own pasta, you won't need this book to help you. So this information is about dried pasta and noodles.

> **Rule of thumb**
> *Allow 4–5oz/100–125g of dried pasta per person for a main course.*

HOW LONG WILL IT TAKE TO COOK?

The instructions ought to be on the packet. But what if you've lost the packet, or it's written in Italian and you can't read it? Brands vary but, in the absence of other directions, this chart should help. For any variety not listed here, just find the most similar one you can. Bear in mind that wholewheat pasta will take a lot longer to cook (and still be virtually uneatable, but that's just my view). Just for fun I've included what the names mean. Cooking times are from when the water comes back to the boil after putting the pasta in.

Variety	Cooking time (mins)	Meaning
Capellini	6	Fine hairs (known as 'angel hair')
Conchiglie, large	14	Shells
Conchiglie, medium or small	10	Shells
Farfalle	12	Butterflies
Fettucine	12	Little ribbons
Fusilli	12	Little spindles
Gnocchi	10	Lumps
Lasagne	5	From the Latin for 'pot'
Linguine	11	Little tongues
Macaroni	14	Unknown (even to Italians)
Manicotti	12	Little muffs
Mostaccioli	14	Little moustaches
Orecchiette	11	Little ears
Penne	11	Quills
Radiatore	10	Radiators
Rigatoni	14	From the Italian for 'grooves'
Rotini	9	Spirals
Ruote	11	Cartwheels
Strozzapreti	11	Priest stranglers
Spaghetti	9	Length of cord
Tagliatelle	7	From the Italian for 'cut'
Vermicelli	6	Little worms
Ziti	14	Bridegrooms

If you have bought fresh pasta and want to know how long to cook it for, you need to take account of the thickness the heat has to penetrate. Fresh pasta cooks quickly and something like tagliatelle or farfalle will cook in 2–3 minutes. Stuffed pastas such as ravioli and tortellini will take around 8 minutes.

Chef's tip

To stop pasta boiling over, grease the top inch of the pan with butter or margarine.

HOW TO STOP PASTA STICKING

There are lots of theories about adding salt and oil, but essentially what you need to do is to encourage the pasta pieces to separate rather than clog together while cooking. You can achieve this in three ways:

- ❍ Allow plenty of water for the pasta to move around in.
- ❍ Keep the water well agitated by boiling it hard, not just simmering.
- ❍ Give it a stir just after you've put it in the water, to separate the pieces, and stir regularly while it cooks.

Once the pasta is cooked, don't leave it sitting in a colander or it will stick together. Toss it in a little butter or olive oil if you're not ready to serve it immediately as this will keep it lubricated.

Rule of thumb

Allow at least two pints/1 litre of water per 4oz/100g of dried pasta, but a minimum of 4 pints/2 litres however little you're cooking.

WHICH KIND OF PASTA WITH WHICH SAUCE?

If you're like me, you'll use whatever pasta you have in the cupboard as often as not, and that's fine. Or just marry your pasta and sauces however you please. But it's true that certain shapes are designed to go with particular types of sauces. So if you're entertaining and want to know the best pasta to go with your home made carbonara sauce, or to add to a tuna and bean casserole, here's a rough guide. It's all down to the shape.

Shape	Type of sauce
Long and thin (eg linguine, spaghetti, tagliatelli)	Light, thin sauces that coat the pasta, such as carbonara, olive oil-based sauces, butter etc
Short and tubular (eg macaroni, penne, rigatoni)	Thick sauces that will fill the tubes, such as bolognese, tomato, cheese, smooth vegetable sauces etc
Shapes (eg conchiglie, farfalle, radiatore)	Textured, lumpy sauces where the chunks get caught in the irregular shapes of the pasta, such as chunky vegetable, seafood or bean sauces

I know spaghetti bolognese breaks these guidelines. That just shows that rules are there to be broken.

Pulses

Broadly speaking pulses are divided into beans, peas and lentils. They generally come either dried or tinned.

Obviously you need to read any instructions that come with them, but generally you can use tinned varieties straight from the tin, while dried pulses need soaking, or cooking in liquid for some time.

Rule of thumb

Soak dried pulses in about three times their own volume of water.

BEANS ➡

There are lots of types of dried beans all of which can be used in soups and casseroles. Most of them need to be washed, then soaked (assume overnight unless otherwise indicated on the packet), and then cooked. Here's a guide to the most common varieties, how long they take to cook, and how to use them.

Variety	Cooking time	Uses
Aduki	40 mins	Soups, salads, red bean paste for filling pancakes
Black	1 hour	Salads, soups, stews and good with rice. A good substitute for red kidney beans
Black-eyed	$1^1/_2$ hours	Mostly used in Indian, African and Carribean cooking
Borlotti	$1^1/_2$ hours	Used in Italian cooking for salads, soups and pasta dishes

Butter	1¹/₂ hours	Good in mixed bean salads and stews
Cannellini	1¹/₂ hours	Soups, stews and casseroles.
Flageolet	1¹/₂ hours	Good in salads
Haricot	1¹/₂ hours	These are what baked beans are. Good for cassoulets, soups, salads or purées
Mung	1 hour	These don't need soaking. Often used sprouted in salads and stir-frys
Pinto	1¹/₂ hours	Used in Mexican cooking, and soups and stews
Red kidney	1¹/₂ hours	The classic ingredient in chilli con carne, they are also good in spicy and hearty stews
Soya	3–4 hours	High in protein (if they've been boiled for a good hour to destroy the substance that inhibits protein absorbtion) but bland, so use in dishes with other stronger flavours

Chef's tip

Don't add salt to dried beans before or during cooking as this can make them tough. If you want to add salt, do it at the end of the cooking process.

TOXIC BEANS

Red kidney beans, traditionally used in chilli con carne among other things, are one of the varieties requiring special treatment. They contain an enzyme which can cause food poisoning. You can prevent this by soaking the dried beans overnight, washing them, and then bringing them to the boil before cooking them at a boil for at least 40 minutes. Alternatively – if you're in a hurry – you can start by boiling them hard for 40 minutes, and then cover and soak them for 4 hours (so still not great if you're in a big hurry).

Tinned varieties should already have been treated so you can use them straight from the tin, but always check the side of the tin for directions. The same applies to aduki, black, black-eyed and soya beans.

PEAS ●──▶

There are three main types of dried peas:

● *Blue peas* (or marrowfat peas) are slightly floury and keep their shape when you cook them.
● *Chick peas* look almost more like a nut, and taste nutty too. They also keep their shape when cooked.
● *Split peas* can be either yellow or green, and taste sweeter than blue or chick peas. They will cook down to a purée well and are often used in soups, or simply served as a purée. They should be soaked first for 1–2 hours, and will then cook in an hour.

LENTILS ●──▶

Dried lentils (unlike peas and beans, I've never seen a fresh lentil) come in a wide range of colours in the green/yellow/red/brown spectrum. If you're wondering whether to use the packet you've just found at the back of the cupboard, the only really significant question (apart from the sell by date) is whether they'll hold their shape or cook down to a purée.

> ## Rule of thumb
> *Green or brown lentils generally retain their shape well when you cook them, while yellow and red lentils usually cook down to a purée.*

You don't need to soak lentils, though you will need to wash them and pick out any discoloured ones. The mushy ones are often used to thicken curries, and all varieties can be used for soups and casseroles.

PUY LENTILS

These dark green lentils are considered to be the most gourmet variety, and are often served as an accompaniment for meat, poultry and fish. They don't need soaking, cook in about half an hour, and hold their shape well.

VARIETIES AND HOW TO COOK THEM

It's a staple food in many parts of the world, so how come lots of us find it so damnably difficult to get right? Part of the solution is to use the right kind of rice for the dish you're cooking. So here's a round up of the most common types, how long they take to cook, and how to use them.

Rice	Cooking time (mins)	Uses
Basmati	20 (boiling)	Indian variety, but actually a great all-rounder and the easiest to cook without the grains sticking together
Brown	40 (boiling)	Only the outer husk is removed so this is very nutritious. Tasty but chewy
Long grain white	20 (boiling)	Well cooked, this is the classic fluffy rice.
Risotto (eg arborio, carnaroli)	25 (boiling)	Named because it's ideal in risotto as it can absorb masses of liquid without cooking down to mush
Short grain	$1^1/_2$ hrs (in the oven)	Pudding rice. Sticks because it's very starchy, which makes it good for puddings
Sticky	15–20 (steaming)	Another pudding variety that is used in chinese cooking. It's easier to pick up with chopsticks because it's sticky

Thai fragrant	20–25 (boiling)	Mildly fragrant long grained variety that is slightly sticky, and used in Thai cooking
Wild	50 (boiling)	Technically a grass seed rather than a rice. It's dark brown and hard work to eat on its own but very tasty mixed in with another variety. Sometimes used as the basis of stuffing for poultry

Rule of thumb
Allow about 3oz/75g rice per serving.

HOW TO STOP RICE STICKING ——▶

Some varieties, of course, are supposed to be sticky. But if you want your rice to come out fluffy with all the grains easily separated, here's what to do:

- ◐ start with a rice such as long grain white or basmati which is low in starch
- ◐ use plenty of water
- ◐ keep the rice boiling well (but not overly fast) so the grains are agitated, and the starch is well dispersed in the water
- ◐ don't overcook it

You can cook fluffy rice using what is known as the 'absorbtion method' but if you haven't yet perfected unsticky rice by boiling you might want to wait before you progress to this. The idea, if you do it (and it does retain more flavour and nutrients) is:

◐ measure water to three times the volume of the rice and bring it to the boil in a pan with a tight-fitting lid
◐ when it comes to the boil, add the rice
◐ as soon as it comes back to the boil, reduce the heat
◐ boil it for 15 minutes without lifting the lid (losing the steam messes up the timing)
◐ at the end of this time the rice should have absorbed all the water and be fluffy and cooked

Or, of course, burnt to the bottom of the pan which you couldn't have checked for as you're not supposed to lift the lid. That's why this is the advanced method. Practise it on the family before cooking it for guests you want to impress.

For how to salvage sticky or burnt rice, see page 144.

Grains

Occasionally you may find yourself taken with an urge to cook something rustic sounding like buckwheat, or to find a use for that half packet of millet left over from some recipe you've forgotten. If you're not in the habit of cooking with a particular grain you may not know what to do with it. So here's a basic rundown.

BARLEY

Pearl barley can be added to soups and stews (such as Scotch broth) and will cook to tender in about an hour. It has a slightly nutty taste and is slightly chewy. Barley meal and barley flour can be added to wheat flour when you're making bread.

BUCKWHEAT

This is traditional in blinis and can be used for pancakes. It's also good in rice dishes and stuffings.

BULGAR WHEAT

This is pre-cooked cracked wheat. You can use it as you would rice, and it's the basis of the Lebanese salad tabbouleh. As it's already cooked it only needs rehydrating by covering with hot water for about 25 minutes.

CORN AND POLENTA

You can use cornmeal to make corn bread. It's also sold as polenta, which you put in boiling water and simmer until it is the consistency of porridge. This takes about 45 minutes, although you can get quick-cook varieties that take only 7 or 8 minutes. It's almost completely tasteless, but a good vehicle for other flavours such as butter, olive oil or herbs. If you leave it to go cold you can slice it and grill or fry it.

Coarse ground corn meal is sometimes called hominy. Cornflour is used as a thickening agent, usually combined with a little cold water and then added to whatever you're trying to thicken, generally at the end of the cooking process.

COUSCOUS

This is actually grains of semolina coated in flour. It's a traditional Moroccan staple, cooked and served with meat or vegetable stews or tagines. Traditionally couscous is steamed more than once. However you're likely to have bought ready-steamed couscous. Follw the directions on the packet assuming you have them; it's likely you just need to add boiling water and leave for about 10 minutes until the couscous grains swell.

MILLET

You can use this like brown rice. If you have flakes you can add these to soups and stews.

OATMEAL

This very Scottish grain comes in three grades: coarse (or pinhead), medium and fine.

- ◑ Pinhead oatmeal is good in soups and stews.
- ◑ Medium is used for porridge (it needs plenty of soaking first) or combined with wheat flour for breadmaking.
- ◑ Fine oatmeal can go into scones and biscuits.

RYE

You're likely to buy this as rye flour, which goes into bread. It can replace wheat flour or be used with it. Coarse ground rye flour is used in pumpernickel bread. You might also get rye flakes, which can be used as porridge (much like oat flakes) or in muesli.

SAGO

This is the starchy stem of the sago palm formed into pearls. It is cooked similarly to pudding rice.

SEMOLINA

This is a by-product of the wheat milling process, and is used to produce couscous (see above). Medium ground semolina is often used to make puddings, rather like a pudding rice. The fine ground variety is an ingredient of a type of Italian gnocchi.

TAPIOCA

This is very similar to sago (see above) and is made from the root of the cassava plant.

WHEAT BRAN

This is one of the most nutritious parts of the wheat grain, and one that is removed in refining wheat flour. You can add it to bread or sprinkle it on cereal.

WHEAT GERM

Another healthy part of the wheat grain lost in the refining process. Add it to cereal or yoghurt. You can buy it toasted or raw; keep the raw stuff in the fridge or it will go off quickly.

Very broadly flours are divided into two types, soft and hard, or strong. Soft flour is used to make cakes and biscuits because it is light. Strong flour is heavier, and is used for breadmaking because the gluten in it is able to stretch and incorporate the air bubbles needed in a yeast dough. Here are the main flours you may have in your cupboard, and what to use them for. You may have flours that combine some of these terms, such as strong wholemeal flour, or plain white flour.

- ◑ *Plain* flour is almost always made from soft wheat in the UK, and produces a really crumbly texture. It is ideal for biscuits, shortcrust pastry and sauces.
- ◑ *Self-raising* flour is made from soft wheat and has had raising agents added to it so that whatever you cook with it will rise – cakes, scones and pastry. You can use

it in place of plain flour + baking powder, if that's what your recipe calls for.

○ *Strong* flour comes from hard wheat varieties and therefore is perfect for producing an elastic dough. It is perfect for breadmaking (it's often labelled as 'bread flour') and is also good for puff, flaky and choux pastry.

○ *White* flour has been refined to remove the coarser particles of wheat, and give a lighter flour which is – as its name suggests – pretty well white. It can be strong, plain or self-raising.

○ *Wholemeal* flour is made using the whole grain of wheat, and therefore contains more fibre and is healthier than white flour. It can be soft or strong, plain or self-raising, and is always heavier than the equivalent white flour. You can mix it half and half with white flour to get the health benefits with a lighter texture. You can use it for pastry, cakes, bread, biscuits and sauces.

Eggs

— Uncooked eggs —

STORING EGGS

Eggs are best kept out of the fridge in a cool larder, pointed end down. Aim to use them within a fortnight of buying them. Separated whites or yolks can be kept, covered, in a fridge for up to 24 hours.

I should say that current health and safety advice is to keep eggs in the fridge. However, if you do this take them out of the fridge an hour or two before you use them if you're planning to boil them (otherwise the shell is more likely to crack on contact with the boiling water), or before baking. Also, don't store them near anything smelly (such as onions) as the porous shells will absorb any strong smells.

HOW TO TELL IF AN EGG IS FRESH

Before you break an egg, you can still test whether it is fresh. An egg has an air space at the blunt end which gets bigger with age. So put it in a bowl of water and see what happens:

It lies flat on the bottom	Fresh
It stays on the bottom but one end tilts up	Not so fresh
It floats	Break it open warily; it may be bad

Once you've broken an egg open, a fresh egg will have a rounder yolk, and the white will cling to the yolk rather than running away from it.

Chef's tip

If you get a small amount of yolk in your egg white, the easiest way to remove it is with a piece of eggshell.

How to tell whether an egg is raw or hardboiled ●──◗

It's easy to do, especially if there's more than one cook in the family – someone leaves an egg lying around the kitchen and you don't know whether it has been cooked or not. All you have to do is spin it (not too close to the edge of the worksurface in case it turns out not to be cooked). If it spins evenly, it's hard boiled. If the spin is wobbly, it's uncooked.

As a double check put your finger on the egg to stop the spinning, and then remove it. If it starts spinning again slowly it must be raw – in other words the yolk and white inside haven't quite stopped spinning independently so they restart when you lift your finger.

➤ *Cooking eggs* ➤

HOW LONG SHOULD YOU BOIL AN EGG? ➤

It's just so tricky because you can't actually look inside
an egg to see how well cooked it is. The precise time
depends of course in part on how hard you boil it. The following times assume that you put the egg in boiling water
and bring it quickly back to a very gentle simmer. From
that point, here's a guide to timings:

Soft boiled	5 minutes
Medium boiled	7 minutes
Hard boiled	10 minutes

If you prefer to boil your eggs hard (ie a rolling boil rather
than a simmer), this is a better gauge of how long they
will take to cook:

Soft boiled	3 minutes
Medium boiled	$4^1/_2$ minutes
Hard boiled	10 minutes

Whichever method you use, hard boiled eggs should be
put straight into cold water after cooking or the heat
inside them will continue the cooking process. That's
when you get that nasty greenish coating to the yolk.

Rule of thumb
*You can't cook scrambled eggs too slowly, or an
omlette too quickly.*

Eggs from other birds ●━━▶

DUCK EGGS

Duck eggs have a richer, more gamey flavour than hens' eggs. The yolk is yellower and the white more rubbery when it's fried. They are larger than hens' eggs.

◐ Soft boil in 6–8 minutes
◐ Hard boil in 15 minutes

GOOSE EGGS

Goose eggs are much more flavoursome and richer than hens' eggs. They make very good scrambled eggs and omlettes.

◐ Soft boil in 10 minutes
◐ Hard boil in 18 minutes

QUAIL EGGS

These taste a little more gamey than hens' eggs and are much smaller (the Japanese quail's egg is smaller than the Italian quail's). They are most often served boiled, frequently as a starter, for example with crème fraîche and caviar, or in salads.

◐ Soft boil in 2–3 minutes
◐ Hard boil in 5 minutes

Dairy products

— Milk —

Not hard to get your head round the idea of milk generally, but just for the record here are the basic types available. Where it isn't completely obvious I've indicated how you might use them.

○ **Buttermilk** is what's left of cream after butter has been churned from it. About the only thing you're likely to use it for normally is making scones.

○ **Condensed milk** comes in a can. It is sweetened and homogenised (see below) and has been heat treated. It is then evaporated down to a third of its original volume. It's used in ice creams, puddings and sweet sauces.

○ **Evaporated milk** also comes in a can. It differs from condensed milk in two ways: it is not quite so concentrated, and it isn't sweetened. You can use it as an alternative to pouring cream (if you're truly desperate) or in ice creams, puddings and milk puddings.

○ **Goat's milk** is easier to digest than cow's milk, and is suitable for some people who have an intolerance to cow's milk. The flavour is different and very pleasant though it may take some getting used to. You can use it just as you would cow's milk.

○ **Homogenised milk** has been treated so that the

cream (or fat content) is distributed evenly throughout the milk rather than coming to the surface.

- **Semi-skimmed milk** has had some of the fat skimmed off so the fat content is about 50% that of whole milk.

- **Skimmed milk** has had almost all the fat removed. This means it also loses the fat soluble vitamins A and D, though in other ways it is more nutritious than whole milk. It is not recommended for children under five.

- **Soya milk** is made from soya beans. You can use it as a milk substitute for anyone who doesn't consume dairy products or is lactose-intolerant. It is slightly nutty and thicker than normal milk. It splits if you put it into hot drinks, though this doesn't alter the flavour (sadly).

- **Sterilised/UHT (ultra heat treated) milk** has been treated to destroy just about all bacteria so it lasts a very long time: several months outside a fridge so long as you don't open it. It doesn't taste great but is fine for emergencies.

- **Whole milk** is just proper milk.

Cream

Most cream doesn't need much explanation, but a couple of types may do:

- **Clotted cream** is made by gently heating it to create a yellow crust. It could theoretically be whipped but it doesn't need to be as it is already thick. It isn't used for cooking because it separates when you heat it.

- **Crème fraiche** is fresh cream which has been slightly soured and also thickened (using particular bacteria). It is served with puddings and also used to make dips and salad dressings. You can add it to sauces and casseroles to give them a creamier taste. It can be substituted with creamy natural fromage frais at a pinch if necessary (see below under cheese).

◦ **Smetana** is a low fat soured cream (originally from Russia).

◦ **Soured cream** has been artificially soured (but, unlike crème fraîche, not thickened). It is more sour than crème fraîche. I can't tell you why anyone would go out of their way to make cream sour, but they do. It is used to add flavour and richness to savoury dishes such as soups and casseroles, and in salad dressings and dips.

Chef's tip

◦ *You can only whip cream that is labelled either 'double' or 'whipping' cream, as other varieties don't have a high enough fat content.*

◦ *If you boil a liquid that contains cream there is a risk the cream may curdle, especially if the liquid also contains anything acidic such as lemon juice.*

Butter

Like milk, butter is pretty easy to use too. Just a couple of points you might find useful:

◦ **Clarified butter** has had the milk solids removed – this is what ghee is – so it can be used for frying at higher temperatures as it burns less easily. However it doesn't impart such a good flavour.

◦ **Salted butter** keeps better than unsalted.

◦ **Unsalted butter** is better for frying as it doesn't burn so readily.

Chef's tip

If your butter is too hard to spread straight from the fridge, either put in in a microwave for a few seconds or slice it with a cheese slicer.

❦— *Cheese* —❦

Most cheeses are easy to use: you just eat them as they are. Or maybe with some crackers, chutney or grapes. If you want to put together a cheese board go for variety: one hard cheese, one blue, one soft, one goat's cheese or whatever you please. Three is plenty, more than five is unnecessary.

Chef's tip

Never serve cheese straight from the fridge. It needs to be at room temperature to bring out the flavour. If you store it in the fridge, take it out at least an hour before serving.

It's when you start using cheese in cooking that it can get confusing. Which is the one you use in cheesecake? Moussaka? Fondue? Here's a rundown of the main cheeses used in cooking and what you might need to know about them.

- ○ **Cream cheese** is a soft, very creamy cheese (the name may have given you a clue there) which is used to make cheesecake as well as other desserts, and the topping for carrot cake.
- ○ **Curd cheese** is very similar to cream cheese but lower in fat and slightly acid in flavour. It can be used

for dips, and blends well into soups and sauces. It is also used in some desserts including cheesecake.

- ◐ **Emmental** is the Swiss one with holes in that goes stringy when melted. It's the most commonly used ingredient in fondue.
- ◐ **Fromage blanc** is very like fromage frais (see next entry) but a smoother texture.
- ◐ **Fromage frais** is similar in consistency to very thick cream, and tastes a bit like yoghurt. You can buy loads of flavoured varieties in pots, just like yoghurt. You can also get natural fromage frais which makes good dips and dressings. It is not dissimilar to crème fraîche (see above under cream). It can be used to replace cream and yoghurt in cooking as it is less likely to curdle.
- ◐ **Gruyère** is similar to Emmental and likewise good melted in fondue.
- ◐ **Halloumi** is most commonly served cooked, as it retains its shape when fried or grilled. It's quite a chewy cheese, usually made from ewe's milk, though some varieties combine ewe's, goat's and cow's milk.
- ◐ **Mascarpone** is a yellowish creamy smooth cheese which is almost sweet. Consequently it is used to make puddings such as tiramisu, or is served as an accompaniment with fruit. It melts down to an incredibly rich, creamy sauce – just add some parmesan if you want a stronger flavour and use it in lasagne or moussaka.
- ◐ **Mozzarella** is the really stretchy cheese you get on top of pizza. When cold, it's often put together with tomato, basil and perhaps avocado to make a Mediterranean salad. It is traditionally made from buffalo milk, though often nowadays it's made using cow's milk. It comes in balls which are packaged in plastic

bags or pots containing water. This is necessary to keep the cheese fresh because it has no rind.

◐ **Parmesan** is very hard and delicious either as it is, or shaved or grated over Italian pasta dishes. It's also good in sauces along with milder cheeses. Its Italian name is *parmigiano reggiano*.

◐ **Pecorino** is similar to parmesan and can be used in the same way.

◐ **Quark** is a kind of curd cheese with a mild taste; it's similar to yoghurt or fromage frais, but has a richer taste if you use it in cooking. You can add it to soups and sauces, make dips and dressings with it, or serve it as an accompaniment to puddings.

◐ **Ricotta** is similar to mascarpone (see above) but grainier in texture. It is slightly less rich and creamy (and lower in fat), and similarly faintly sweet. It cooks well and is ideal for dishes such as moussaka. It's also traditionally paired with spinach.

Sauces, dressings and flavourings

Sauces

Perhaps the most commonly cooked sauces of all are white sauce (béchamel) and cheese sauce. As a result these are both included in the classic recipes in the back of the book, along with gravy. There are a few other sauces you may want a reminder of the quantities for (this isn't a cookbook so I'm assuming you know how to make them). So here they are:

MAYONNAISE

2 egg yolks
1 tsp white wine vinegar
$^1/_2$pt/250ml oil

...plus any mustard, seasoning or whatever you like. Olive oil is rather too strong; sunflower or grapeseed are good. Make sure all the ingredients are at room temperature before you start. For how to rescue a curdled mayonnaise, see page 140.

VARIATIONS ON MAYONNAISE

- ◐ *Aioli* add 4 crushed garlic cloves to the egg yolks.
- ◐ *Rouille* add 4 crushed garlic cloves, $^1/_2$ tspn cayenne pepper and a pinch of saffron to the egg yolks.
- ◐ *Tartare* after making the mayonnaise, add 1oz/25g each of chopped gherkins and chopped capers, and 2tbspns chopped parsley.

HOLLANDAISE ⊶

1 tblspn white wine vinegar
$^1/_2$ tspn crushed peppercorns
1 tblspn water
2 egg yolks
8oz/200g clarified melted butter

For how to rescue a curdled Hollandaise, see page 140.

VARIATIONS ON HOLLANDAISE

Bearnaise add 2 tblspns chopped tarragon and 2 chopped shallots to the vinegar reduction at the beginning. Stir in a further tblspn of chopped tarragon and one of chervil before serving.

Chef's tip

To stop a warm sauce developing a skin if you're not serving it immediately, take a square of greaseproof paper larger than the diameter of the saucepan:

- ◐ *Fold it in half, then in half again, then fold this over to make a triangle, and keep folding two or three more times until you have a very long thin triangle.*
- ◐ *Hold the central point of this over the middle of the*

pan, and mark the point along the triangle where the edge of the pan comes to.

◐ Now cut or tear along this line, and cut off the very tip of the triangle.

◐ Open the whole thing out and you should have a circle (near as dammit) the same size as your pan, with a small hole in the centre. Lay this over the sauce – the hole allows for evaporation.

MINT SAUCE

4oz/100g fresh mint
1 tblspn caster sugar
2 tblspns malt vinegar

BREAD SAUCE

$^1/_2$pt/375ml milk
1 small onion
6 cloves
1oz/25g fresh breadcrumbs

...and whatever seasoning you want to add.

PESTO

3oz/75g fresh basil leaves
2 crushed garlic cloves
1 tblspn chopped pine nuts
2 tblspns freshly grated parmesan
$^1/_2$pt/125ml extra virgin olive oil

THICKENING SAUCE

If you're devising your own sauce, or you're following a recipe but can't get the sauce as thick as you'd like, you can thicken it in a number of ways. The two simplest are making a roux or using a thickening agent.

MAKING A ROUX ●━━━◗

This involves mixing melted butter and flour and then adding the liquid to it. Melt the butter in a pan until it foams, add an equal quantity of flour, and stir in for about 45 seconds before adding the liquid. As a rough guide allow 1oz/25g each of butter and flour to $^1/_2$ pint/250ml of sauce.

THICKENING AGENTS ●━━━◗

Cornflour and arrowroot are the most common thickeners. If you have a choice, use cornflour for sweet sauces and arrowroot for savoury ones. Unlike a roux made with wheat flour, these won't turn a clear sauce cloudy. Allow about a teaspoon of either to 200ml (just under $^1/_2$ pint) of sauce. Mix it with a little water, then whisk it into the sauce. Bring it to the boil and simmer for a couple of minutes until it thickens. Then take it off the heat or the sauce may thin again.

HOW THICK SHOULD IT BE? ●━━━◗

If you're making a thickened sauce such as a béchamel and the recipe calls for it to be thin, medium or thick, what does it mean?

◐ *Thin* This should be like single cream. When it covers the back of the wooden spoon you should be able to draw a cross in the sauce with your finger that only just holds.
◐ *Medium* This should comfortably coat the back of the spoon, but still be runny.
◐ *Thick* You should be able to pick this up in a lump on the spoon, but it should still flow off the spoon if you tap it on the edge of the pan.

Dressings

BLUE CHEESE

8 tblspns soured cream
4oz/100g cream cheese
4oz/100g double cream
4oz/100g crumbled blue cheese

Whizz the whole lot together in a blender, and thin with milk if you want to.

CAESAR DRESSING

1 crushed garlic clove
4 chopped anchovy fillets
4 tblspns lemon juice
1 tspoon English mustard
1 egg yolk
$1/_2$pint/250ml olive oil

Blend everything except the oil. Then drizzle in the oil as you would with mayonnaise. (For the ingredients of a classic Caesar salad, see page 113.)

ROSE MARIE SAUCE

Equal quantities of mayonnaise and tomato ketchup.

VINAIGRETTE

- Use a ratio of oil:vinegar of about 3:1 as a general guide. However you may want more oil if the vinegar is very strongly flavoured, or if the salad contains very bitter leaves.
- Use a good quality oil such as olive or sunflower, and a red or white wine vinegar. Obviously depending on what you're serving it with you may like to replace this

with a raspberry vinegar or balsamic (though this can discolour the salad leaves).

◐ If you like to sweeten your vinaigrette, you'll find that runny honey rather than sugar helps it to emulsify better (ie stops the oil and vinegar separating so readily). A spoonful of Dijon mustard has the same effect.

◐ Dress the salad just before serving so the dressing doesn't discolour it. Make sure the leaves are dry or the water will reject the dressing.

⊚— *Flavourings* —⊛

You are of course perfectly at liberty to use any flavouring you like with any food, and you may come up with some inventive and delicious combinations. So what follows is not prescriptive in any way, but simply an indication of the traditional pairings of flavours and foods which you may want a reminder of.

HERBS ——▶

◐ **Basil** pairs brilliantly with tomato, and is at its best raw in salads. Use whole or torn leaves rather than chopping it.

◐ **Bayleaf** goes best with fish and poultry, or cook it in soups and stews. Remove the leaf before serving.

◐ **Chervil** tastes rather like a cross between tarragon and parsley. It goes particularly well with poultry, fish and eggs.

◐ **Chives** are mildly oniony and go well sprinkled raw on eggs, cheese, fish or in salads. Cut them with scissors rather than a knife; it's much easier.

- **Coriander** Fresh coriander goes well with fish, cheese and egg dishes. Or sprinkle it raw over curries. (Also see coriander seeds below under spices.)
- **Dill** is particularly good for fish, salads and dressings.
- **Fennel leaves** are used fresh to flavour egg and fish dishes, and in salads and dressings. They are quite strongly flavoured (of aniseed) so use sparingly.
- **Lavender** flowers are used sparingly in ice cream, milk-based puddings and biscuits.
- **Lemon grass** is especially popular in Thai cooking. Remove any damaged leaves and chop or thinly slice the stalk.
- **Lovage** has a very strong celery taste and goes well (in modest quantities) in vegetable dishes especially.
- **Marjoram** goes with meat and poultry, and particularly well with tomatoes.
- **Mint** is great with peas or potatoes, in dressings and of course in mint sauce (see page 99).
- **Oregano** is similar to marjoram and is most often used in Italian pasta dishes, especially paired with tomato.
- **Parsley** comes chiefly in curly and flat-leaved (Italian) varieties. The flat-leaved is stronger flavoured. It's particularly good with fish and eggs, and in parsley sauce for ham (just a basic white sauce with masses of chopped parsley added). Chewed fresh it supposedly freshens the breath even after eating garlic – you'll have to test it for yourself.
- **Rosemary** is evergreen so it's fresh all year round. It goes with most things but is especially good with roast lamb and with root vegetables.
- **Sage** is traditionally used with meat and poultry – especially in stuffings – and with eggs. It can be a little bitter if you use too much.

○ *Savory* goes best with poultry, eggs and rice.
○ *Tarragon* is especially good with fish and poultry, often used in wine or cream sauces.
○ *Thyme* is a real all-rounder and goes with just about anything. Being evergreen it's also available fresh all year round.

Rule of thumb

Avoid dried herbs if you possibly can. The flavour just isn't as good. Either use herbs in season or chop fresh herbs and pack them into an ice tray. Cover with water and freeze. Then add a cube or two to soups and stews through the winter.

WHAT IS IN A BOUQUET GARNI?

You can put pretty much what you please in this little packet of flavouring for soups and stews. Traditionally however it consists of parsley stalks, thyme and a bay leaf. Wrap these in a leek leaf or a stick of celery, tie with string and put in the pot. Leave the other end of the string tied loosely to the handle so you can fish the whole thing out easily later.

SPICES ◆━━▶

○ *Allspice berries* (it's also available ground) taste similar to cloves. Use whole in chutneys and pickles, stews etc. Use ground with apple and in cakes and puddings.
○ *Aniseed* tastes similar to liquorice and is most often used in baking.
○ *Caraway seed* is used in rye bread and goes well with pork. It's also good in coleslaw.
○ *Cardamom seeds* need to be removed from the

pods as a rule, since the pods are too tough to make pleasant eating. They go best in cakes and biscuits.

- **Cayenne pepper** is made from ground dried red chilli peppers so it's very hot. Use it sparingly in curries and spicy dishes.
- **Celery seeds** taste stronger than fresh celery. They go well with beef, lamb, and vegetable stews and soups.
- **Chilli powder** is very hot so use it sparingly in curries, breads, and dips, dressings and barbecue sauces.
- **Cinnamon** goes best with sweet dishes, especially with cooked fruits. Use it ground, or steep the sticks in liquid and then remove them – for example, steep them in the milk for ice creams or in mulled wine.
- **Cloves** are used in bread sauce and to stud baked hams, and pair well with cooked apples. They're not very pleasant to eat so you need to use them ground, or remove whole cloves before serving.

Chef's tip

If you want a clove flavour but don't want to spend ages picking the cloves out of your apple pie or whatever, use ground allspice instead.

- **Coriander seeds** go well ground or crushed in curries and beef dishes (also see fresh coriander above under herbs).
- **Cumin** seeds go well, whole or ground, in curries and with potatoes.
- **Fennel seeds** go well in curries and stews. They can also be used in breads and salads.
- **Fenugreek seeds** are used widely in Indian curries.
- **Ginger** can be fresh or ground. Peel the skin off fresh ginger and then chop it finely. It is extremely strong

when raw, though much milder once it's cooked. Add fresh or dried ginger to oriental dishes, stir frys and also sweet dishes, breads and cakes. Stem ginger (which comes in syrup) is very sweet; the liquid on its own makes a good flavouring.

◐ *Juniper berries* are most commonly paired, crushed or whole, with game. They are also used to flavour gin, incidentally.

◐ *Mace* comes from the same plant as nutmeg and tastes similar but milder. It goes well with poultry and fish, and cheese dishes.

◐ *Nutmeg* is generally used ground, though you can buy it whole and grate it yourself. It's good with beef, cheese and in fruit puddings.

◐ *Paprika* is made from dried and ground red peppers. It is used in goulash and potato dishes especially, and to add colour as well as flavour to sauces. It's similar to cayenne but not as strong (remember P for paprika and pepper, C for cayenne and chilli).

◐ *Poppy seeds* are used in cakes and breads, biscuits and in salad dressings.

◐ *Saffron* should be used sparingly. It flavours and colours chicken, rice and seafoods. It is famously derived from crocuses and is more valuable, weight for weight, than gold.

◐ *Sesame seeds* have a very mild flavour. You can use them in stir-frys or in breads.

◐ *Star anise* can be used whole or ground in Chinese and Indian dishes.

◐ *Tamarind* is sold as a sour-tasting paste (slightly like lemon juice) which is used in Indian cooking. You can use lemon juice as a substitute if you're fresh out of tamarind.

- ◑ **Turmeric** is quite peppery and very yellow. It goes well in curries and also in egg or chicken dishes.
- ◑ **Vanilla** comes in a pod or as a liquid extract and is used to flavour sweet dishes

CURRY SPICES

You can buy ground curry powders which are a blend of several traditional curry spices. These come in mild, medium and hot varieties, and you can also get (along with more specialist varieties):

- ◑ **Korma** A mild, sweet spice, often combined with almond and coconut flavours.
- ◑ **Madras** A hot blend of spices: best with red meats.
- ◑ **Garam masala** A hot spice blend used in various types of curry.
- ◑ **Chinese five spice** This powder has a strong aniseed flavour. It's used to flavour meat and poultry and in marinades. It's great with pork.

OIL ⚊➡

There are countless oils you can use for flavouring dressings or garnishing soups, some of which are made from a base oil flavoured with truffle, lemon or whatever, and others which are extracted from a plant. Here though are the most common oils used for cooking.

- ◑ **Corn** This oil is often used for deep frying because it smokes at a very high temperature. It's very cheap and can leave an unpleasant cooking smell.
- ◑ **Grapeseed** is a mild, aromatic oil (a by-product of wine making). Good in salads and for mayonnaise.
- ◑ **Groundnut** This comes from peanuts, of course, and is often thought second only to olive oil for cooking. The flavour is very delicate.

○ **Olive** Famously good for you, this is arguably the only oil you should use in cooking as others release unhealthy free radicals when heated (others are fine for dressings). It can become bitter after opening so buy smaller bottles if you don't use it often. Extra virgin olive oil is green and strong tasting; it's made from the first pressing. Subsequent pressings produce lighter, paler, less flavoursome (and less expensive) oil. You can cook with light olive oil.

○ **Rapeseed** This pale oil is also known as canola. It is used for frying and salads, especially in the East and Mediterranean.

○ **Safflower** This is a good all-purpose oil. The taste is very mild, and as safflower oil is low in unsaturated fats it is often recommended with low-cholesterol diets.

○ **Sesame** A dark oil made from toasted sesame seeds – the darker the colour, the stronger the flavour. It burns easily so isn't generally used for frying.

○ **Sunflower** A good all-purpose oil. You can combine it with olive oil to add flavour for dressings and mayonnaise.

○ **Vegetable** Oil sold under this name is a blend of several bland oils. It is best for cooking, where it can be heated to high temperatures.

○ **Walnut** You can't really cook with this as it doesn't stand the heat, but it's a very nutty flavoursome oil for salads. It doesn't keep well so buy a small bottle and keep it in the fridge.

VINEGAR ━━◀

The word vinegar literally means 'sour' or 'sharp' wine, and it's made by an acid fermentation of fresh alcohol. So wine vinegar is made from wine, cider vinegar from cider, malt vinegar from malted barley and so on. So by and large this should give you a pretty good idea of both quality and flavour. Cider vinegar goes well with apple-based dishes (surprise, surprise), perry vinegar with pears and so on.

Flavoured vinegars are usually made from wine vinegar and have had herbs or other flavourings steeped in them. So you can buy tarragon vinegar, garlic vinegar, raspberry vinegar and so on (or indeed make them yourself).

Here's a guide to which vinegar to use when:

Use	Suitable vinegars
Drizzling over cooked meat and fish	Balsamic (you can get white balsamic vinegar), malt on fish and chips
Marinades	Balsamic, cider, light malt, perry, wine, sherry
Oriental cooking	Rice
Pickling	Cider, distilled malt, malt
Salad dressing	Balsamic, champagne, cider, light malt, perry, sherry, wine
Sauces	Light malt, rice, sherry, wine

Chef's tip

Balsamic vinegar is made from special grapes which are harvested late so they have a very high sugar content and lots of flavour. There's a great deal of difference (in price as well as taste) between a cheap balsamic vinegar and the real thing. If you want to buy the good stuff it should say 'of Modena' on it, which is the town in Italy where it is produced.

MUSTARD ●——▶

If you want to add a touch of mustard flavouring to what you're cooking, you may understandably be unsure what kind to use. So here's a quick rundown.

SMOOTH MUSTARDS

These come in a jar and the critical thing to know is how hot they are:

○ **English mustard** is the hot one, great with beef, sausages and cheese. You can cook with it (Welsh rarebit for example) but it will lose its strength if you cook it for too long. Add it near the end of the cooking time.

○ **French mustard** is milder, and the most popular variety is Dijon mustard (Dijon being the mustard capital of the world). It's the mustard to choose for mayonnaise, dressings, and milder creamy sauces for eggs, fish and white meats. A spoonful in cheese sauce brings out the flavour.

WHOLEGRAIN MUSTARDS

Mustards such as Moutarde de Meaux are made from partly crushed seeds and have a grainy, crunchy texture. They come in varying strengths so read the jar. They are good with cold meats and wonderful in potato salads and dressings.

MUSTARD POWDER

This is hot. It can be mixed into a smooth English mustard by mixing it in equal quantities with cold water and leaving it to stand for a few minutes. Then use as for smooth mustard. Never add hot water as this will bring out bitter flavours. In cooking you can often add the powder from the tin without bothering to make it up first.

MUSTARD SEEDS

- **Black mustard seeds** are hot. They are used in Indian cooking and you can crush them and add them to meat dishes. They go particularly well with pork and kidneys.
- **White mustard seeds** are cooler. These are the ones used in pickles and chutneys, and you can crush them and add them to vegetable dishes.

OTHER FLAVOURINGS ━━━▶

- **Fish sauce** is used widely in Thai cooking, not only with fish dishes – it's name relates to the ingredients (it's made from fermented prawns or fish).
- **Hoisin sauce** is made from soya beans, garlic, chilli and spices, and therefore needs to be used sparingly. It is particularly eaten with Peking duck.
- **Mirin** is a sweetened rice wine used in Japanese cooking.
- **Oyster sauce** is a rich, salty, brown sauce made from oysters which is used to add flavour to Chinese food.
- **Soy sauce** is salty and strongly flavoured, and comes in light or rich varieties. Both the Chinese and Japanese use it extensively in cooking, and it's also good in barbecue sauces. You can sprinkle it over rice dishes.

Salads

Salad leaves

You've bought the green salad ingredients, and now you can't remember which leaves are crunchy, which are bitter and so on. Obviously you can just taste them, but to save you the trouble – or to help out before you buy them – here are the most common leaves and their basic flavours.

Taste	Salad leaves
Mild	Iceberg lettuce, lamb's lettuce, little gem, oak leaf, spinach, sweet romaine
Bitter	Chicory, endive, frisée, radicchio
Peppery	Mizuna, red mustard, roccolla, rocket, watercress
Nutty	Cos lettuce, lamb's lettuce
Crunchy	Crispheart lettuce, iceberg lettuce, little gem, sweet romaine

Classic salads

There's always scope for a good argument over what are the classic ingredients of a Caesar salad. So if only for the fun of fuelling the debate, here are the basic components of a few classic salads. You'll never get all the experts to agree, but what follows is as good an answer as any.

CAESAR SALAD

- cos lettuce
- freshly grated or shaved parmesan cheese
- croûtons

And that's it. Other ingredients are often included, especially anchovies (which are a standard part of the salad but classically go in the dressing – see page 101) and eggs.

COLESLAW

All you need to know here is the basic proportion: 4 parts cabbage to 1 part carrot (by weight). It's considered acceptable to bind these with mayonnaise, natural yoghurt or fromage frais, and of course you might want to add grated onion (though I can't think why), raisins or sesame seeds.

GREEK SALAD

- tomatoes
- feta cheese
- diced cucumber
- pitted black olives

As well as these standard ingredients, some recipes also include red onion, green pepper and oregano.

SALAD NICOISE

- tomatoes
- cooked green beans
- cooked diced potato

- hard boiled eggs
- tuna
- lettuce
- pitted olives
- vinaigrette and seasoning

There are countless different versions of this, but the ingredients above are pretty well what define a Nicoise. It often includes anchovy fillets too, and other popular inclusions are thinly sliced onion, parsley, cucumber and capers.

WALDORF SALAD

- celery
- apple
- walnuts
- mayonnaise

Healthy eating

I could write several books on healthy eating (well, some-one could) so I won't get carried away here. But there are one or two things you might want a quick guide to.

Portion sizes

We're always being told to eat five portions of fruit or veg-etables a day, but how much is a portion? Here's a quick guide to what constitutes a portion of the most common foods. Incidentally this is largely taken from Sally Child and Karen Bali's book *The Art of Hiding Vegetables Sneaky ways to feed your children healthy food* (White Ladder Press £7.99), which also lists portion sizes for children at different ages.

VEGETABLES

Aubergine	$^1/_2$
Baby beetroot	4
Baby sweetcorn cobs	5–6
Beansprouts	2 handfuls
Broccoli	4 florets
Brussels sprouts	8
Carrots, cooked	3 tblspns
Cauliflower	4 florets

Celery	1–2 sticks
Cherry tomatoes	5
Cooked veg eg beans	3–4 tblspns
Courgette	$^1/_2$ large
Cucumber	6 slices
Grated carrot	3 tblspns
Leafy green veg, cooked	3 tblspns
Mushrooms	3–4 tblspns
Parsnip	1 large
Peas	3 tblspns
Pepper, fresh	$^1/_2$–1
Pulses, cooked	1 cup
Salad, mixed	1 cereal bowl
Sliced mushrooms	3 tblspns
Sweetcorn kernels	3 tblspns
Tomato	1 large

FRUIT ➡

Apple	1 large
Apricots, dried	5–6
Avocado	$^1/_2$ lge/1 small
Banana	1 large
Blackberries	4 tblspns
Blackcurrants	4 tblspns
Cherries	10
Fruit juice	4 fl oz/100ml
Fruit salad, fresh	dessert bowl
Grapefruit	$^1/_2$
Grapes	15
Kiwi fruit	2
Mango	$^1/_2$
Melon	4oz/100g

Orange	1 large
Peach/nectarine	1
Pear	1 large
Pineapple, fresh	1 large slice
Plum	2–3
Raisins/sultanas	handful
Raspberries	4 tblspns
Rhubarb, cooked	2 tblspns
Satsuma/clementine	2
Strawberries	6–8
Tinned fruit	1 small tin

Although standard advice is to eat 'five a day', for optimum health you should actually aim for eight portions a day.

Vitamins and minerals

If you're trying to increase your intake of zinc, or give your children more vitamin C, it can be handy to have a guide to the best sources of the most important vitamins and minerals. Obviously I'm not listing obscure or minor sources; this is just for quick reference.

Rule of thumb
Healthy women need around 2,000 kcals (calories) intake a day, and healthy men around 2,500 kcals.

VITAMINS ━━▶

Vitamin	Good for	Best sources
A (retinol)	Eyes, skin	Liver, fish oils, carrots, green leaf vegetables, milk products, egg yolks
B1 (thiamine)	Heart, nervous system, digestion	Liver, yeast, wholegrains, rice, peanuts, milk
B2 (riboflavin)	Skin, nails, hair, digestion	Liver, fish, yeast, milk, cheese, green leaf vegetables
B6	Skin, nervous system, digestion	Pork, chicken, fish, bananas, sholegrains, dried pulses
B12	Blood	Liver, meat, fish, milk, cheese
C (ascorbic acid)	Immune system, lowering cholesterol, healing wounds	Citrus fruits, berries, tomatoes, green vegetables, potatoes
D	Bones and teeth	Oily fish, milk and milk products, natural sunlight
E	Protecting against toxins	Green vegetables, wholegrains, eggs, nuts, soya beans
Folic acid	Blood, pregnancy	Liver, yeast, whole wheat, leafy green

vegetables, carrots,
beans, avocado,
apricots, melon, egg
yolks

MINERALS ⟶

Mineral	Good for	Best sources
Calcium	Bones, teeth, immune system	Milk and dairy products, lean meat, nuts, leafy green vegetables, pulses, oily fish, wholegrains
Iron	Blood and muscles	Lean red meat, offal, oily fish, green vegetables, garlic, figs, apricots, eggs, wholewheat bread
Magnesium	Blood pressure, digestion, bones, teeth and muscles	Bananas, apricots, figs, prunes, raisins, lean meat, brown rice, whole wheat, green leafy vegetables, pulses, milk and yoghurt
Potassium	Fluid balance, heart, muscles.	Most foods other than fats and sugars but can be destroyed by overcooking
Selenium	Liver	Nuts, cheese, watercress

| Zinc | Immune system, skin, libido | Shellfish, lean meat and poultry, cheese, brown rice, wholegrains. |

It can be difficult for the body to absorb iron, but vitamin C helps the process so take both together. For example have a glass of orange juice with your meal.

Rule of thumb

The recommendation is that you drink $1^1/_2$–2 litres of liquids a day, preferably water. Sadly alcohol and caffeine drinks don't count at all.

Entertaining

⟡— *Restricted diets* —⟡

There are many people who avoid certain foods not because of taste but for religious or health reasons. If your guest warns you they're allergic to nuts that's pretty easy to grasp. But what if they tell you that they're vegan or coeliac, or you know they're Muslim or pregnant? This doesn't actually tell you exactly what they can and can't eat. So here's a guide to help you. If your guest has very strict religious beliefs best ask them too, as there are a few stipulations observed by the most orthodox followers that I haven't listed.

	Don't serve them...	*Notes*
Candida (yeast intolerance) sufferers	Bread, mushrooms, fermented drinks	
Coeliacs	Anything made from wheat or rye	Buy gluten-free products. Remember to avoid pasta and beer
Diabetics	Excess salt or sugar	

Hindus	Meat (especially beef) and fish, eggs	
Hypertension sufferers	Salt	
Lactose intolerant people	Dairy products	Ask if goats' milk is OK. Read ingredients – loads of things contain milk powder or whey, including some margarines
Muslims	Alcohol, pork (including bacon, lard etc), non-halal meat, fish without fins or scales (eg shellfish), carnivorous animals	Avoid gelatine – use a vegetarian substitute
Orthodox Jews	Non-kosher meat and meat derivatives, pork, fish without fins or scales, cochineal. Don't serve meat and milk at the same meal, or meat and fish.	Avoid gelatine – use a vegetarian substitute
Pregnant women	Raw or partially cooked eggs, meat or poultry, liver, paté, soft cheese,	Wash fruit and salad vegetables thoroughly

	blue cheese. Use chillis, garlic and rosemary only in moderation.	
Sikhs	Halal and kosher meat, alcohol	
Vegans	Meat, fish, eggs, dairy products, honey	Avoid gelatine – use a vegetarian substitute. You can buy vegan substitues for most dairy products
Vegetarians	Meat or fish	Avoid gelatine – use a vegetarian substitute. You can buy vegan substitues for most dairy products

Wine and cocktails

CHOOSING WINE

So you've got people coming to dinner and you want to give them wine. Good for you. But it can be worrying if you don't know much about it and they're keen drinkers. You don't want to get it wrong. So here are a couple of simple guidelines to keep you safe.

- **Don't buy the very cheapest.** The reason is obvious: duty is based on volume, unlike VAT which is based on price. So on a cheap bottle there's not much value in the wine; as the price rises, so does the quality. You can get a drinkable bottle for £2.95, but if you go up to £5.95 the chancellor doesn't get any more money but you get a much better drink.

◐ _Buy from a big wine chain or a supermarket._ Never before in history has there been such a range of good wines available at such low prices. Companies like Tesco and Oddbins can scour the world, buy in huge quantities, and are fiercely competitive. You may get an uninteresting wine but you won't get a bad one. And you can get something pretty good without going into double figures.

Rule of thumb

You're safe with the traditional 'red with meat, white with fish' rule. However if you can stretch to a bottle of each, the guests can choose for themselves. Treat rosé as white.

SERVING WINE

◐ Broadly speaking you should serve red wine at room temperature and white chilled. Bring red out of a chilly larder about 6 hours before drinking.

◐ Nearly all wines benefit from being opened about 12 hours before drinking.

◐ Small bits of cork can be removed from the glass with a teaspoon, more severe crumbling may need a fine strainer or even the full muslin cloth/funnel/decanter treatment.

◐ Don't play popguns with champagne corks. Remove the cork slowly with an unscrewing action, holding it down. Tilt the glass as you serve to minimise froth.

‿ If you recork an opened bottle fairly tightly it may keep for three or four days, or even longer. This isn't recommended for fine wines, though even these can be better the next day.

Rule of thumb
The classic rule is never to let your guest's glass be less than $^1/_2$ full or more than $^1/_2$ full, but I've never met any host who has ever achieved this.

Chef's tip
You can freeze leftover wine to use later in cooking.

COCKTAILS

Your guest has just asked for a G&T, or a whisky sour. You never drink it yourself so you've no idea what goes into it, or in what proportions. Here are recipes for the most common cocktails that you've a chance of having the ingredients for in the house. There's not a cocktail recipe in the world that someone won't argue with, but these are as good as you'll get.

GIN BASED COCKTAILS

‿ **Gin and tonic (G&T)** One shot of gin to two of tonic water, plus a slice of lemon (or lime) and ice.

‿ **Martini cocktail** One shot of gin over ice, and a dash of French vermouth. You can add a green olive on a stick.

‿ **Tom Collins** One shot of gin, ice, juice of half a lemon and a teaspoon of sugar. Shake (if you have a shaker), pour into the glass and top up with soda water.

WHISKY BASED COCKTAILS

- **Whisky highball** 2 measures of whisky over ice, and top up with soda water or ginger ale.
- **Whisky sour** Two measures of whisky, ice, juice of half a lemon and $1^1/_2$ teaspoons of sugar. Shake (if you can), pour into the glass and top up with soda water. Serve with a slice of orange and/or a cocktail cherry.

CHAMPAGNE BASED COCKTAILS

- **Black velvet** Equal quantities of champagne and stout. Pour them into a bowl and then ladle into champagne flutes.
- **Buck's fizz** Put ice in the glass and quarter fill with fresh squeezed orange juice. Top up with champagne (but don't waste good champagne on it). Serve with a slice of orange.

VODKA BASED COCKTAILS

- **Bloody Mary** Ice and one shot of vodka to two of tomato juice and $^1/_2$ shot of lemon juice. Add tabasco, Worcester sauce, salt and pepper. Technically you should stir it with a stick of celery, should you have one.
- **Vodkatini** As for a Martini cocktail (above) but replace the gin with vodka.

RUM BASED COCKTAILS

- **Daiquiri** 2 shots of white rum, juice of $^1/_2$ a lime and 1 teaspoon sugar syrup (or caster sugar). Shake together with ice.
- **Grenada** Three shots dark rum to one shot Martini rosso (sweet), and juice of $^1/_2$ an orange. Pour over ice and sprinkle with ground cinnamon.

Kitchen equipment

Fridge

WHERE IN THE FRIDGE SHOULD YOU KEEP WHAT?

Your fridge should be at a steady temperature of around 2–3°C. This won't kill off bacteria, but it slows them down considerably so food keeps longer, but not indefinitely. In order to minimise contamination of the contents of the fridge, you're recommended to keep food in a particular way. For example, cooked meat can pick up harmful bacteria from raw meat so shouldn't be kept on the shelf below where it may be dripped on. However raw meat will be cooked, which will kill off any bacteria, so you can keep cooked meat above it without worrying. Here's the general recommended fridge scheme.

Top shelf	*Inside door top*
Dairy – yoghurt, cream, sweet dishes	Butter, cheese
Middle shelf	*Inside door bottom*
Cooked meat, cooked leftovers, mayonnaise	Milk, juice, wine and other drinks
Bottom shelf	
Raw meat and fish	

Crisper
Salad ingredients, berry fruits

Minced meat, offal and seafood are more susceptible to bacteria than large cuts of meat, so keep them near the back where the fridge is coldest.

> **Rule of thumb**
> *Never keep cake, bread or soft biscuits in the fridge as it dries them out and ruins them (I just put that in on the offchance a certain member of my family reads this book).*

HOW LONG WILL IT KEEP?

If you have a 'use by' date you'll know how long you can keep food for. But if you don't, here's a guide to how long you can expect some common types of food to keep in the fridge. All this supposes it starts in good condition and is properly wrapped or packaged.

Butter	8 weeks
Casseroles	2 days
Cheese – hard, unopened	3–6 months
Cheese – soft, unopened	1 month
Cream	5 days
Cured meat – ham, salami etc	2–3 weeks
Eggs	1 month
Fish and other seafoods	3 days
Fruit juice	7–14 days
Gravy/meat juices	1–2 days
Margarine	4 months

Mayonnaise	2 months
Meat – cooked	3 days
Meat – raw cuts	3–5 days
Meat – raw minced (inc sausages), offal	2–3 days
Milk	5–7 days
Oil and cooking fat	4 months
Pasta – cooked	1–2 days
Raw poultry	3 days
Salad dressing	3 months
Salads	3–5 days
Salsa	1 month
Shellfish	2 days
Yoghurt	7–14 days

Rule of thumb

If it's gone a funny colour, smells yukky or is growing mould, ignore this guide and any 'use by' date and don't eat it.

WHAT DO ALL THOSE DATES MEAN?

You've found something in your fridge that is past its 'best before' date. Is it OK to eat it? All those different dates can be confusing, so here's what they mean.

Best before	This is to do with quality, not safety. It's used on foods that are unlikely to be harmful but won't taste as good after this date. The main exception recommended is that you don't eat eggs after their 'best before' date. So it's for guidance rather than instruction.

Use by	This is used for foods that can go off quickly. The advice is not to eat food after this date. Except that you can, however, extend this by freezing food or sometimes by cooking it. Whether freezing or storing, these dates assume you follow all instructions such as 'freeze on day of purchase' or 'once opened eat within 5 days'. This is why the label says 'use by' and not 'eat by'.
Display until	This is advice to shop staff for stock control, not for you. It is not a legal requirement.
Sell by	This is advice to shop staff for stock control, not for you. It is not a legal requirement.

Officially there is no such thing as an 'eat by' date, and food producers and retailers shouldn't use it. If you do ever see it, treat it as a 'use by' date.

Freezer

WHERE IN THE FREEZER SHOULD YOU KEEP WHAT?

As with the fridge, there is a recommended layout for your freezer too to prevent cross-contamination (especially if there's a power failure).

Top drawer	Dairy (ice cream, butter, milk), bread, nuts and herbs

Middle drawer Fruit and vegetables

Bottom drawer Meat, fish and poultry

Rule of thumb
*Don't freeze cheese or coffee as it will ruin the flavour.
You also can't freeze raw salad vegetables, eggs in
their shells (raw or cooked), or raw or boiled potatoes.*

STAR RATINGS

Freezers (including freezer compartments) are allocated
up to three stars which indicate how long food will keep
for. The stars indicate how cold the freezer is, and should
be marked somewhere on the front of your freezer or ice-
box. Frozen food packets tell you how long to keep the
food for in a three, two or one star freezer. However if you
don't have a packet the rule of thumb is:

*	–6°C/21°F	One week
**	–12°C/10°F	One month
***	–18°C/0°F	Three months
****	–18°C/0°F	Three months and suitable for
		freezing down fresh foods

HOW LONG WILL IT KEEP?

If you want to freeze fresh rather than pre-packed food,
here's a guide to roughly how long you can expect to keep
particular foods in a three star freezer.

Bread	3 months
Butter	1 year
Cured meat – ham, salami etc	6 months

Egg whites	1 year
Fish and other seafoods	6 months
Fruit – cooked	9 months
Fruit juice	6 months
Margarine	1 year
Milk	3 months
Raw meat – cuts	6–9 months
Raw meat – minced (inc sausages), offal	2–3 months
Raw poultry	6 months
Shellfish	6 months
Soups and stews	2–3 months
Vegetables – cooked	9 months
Yoghurt	1–2 months

Chef's tip

Food that has been frozen should not be refrozen after defrosting.

Microwave

HOW LONG WILL IT TAKE TO COOK?

This will vary according to the make of microwave cooker you have, but what follows is a rough guide in case you've lost the manual that came with it. These timings are all for a 'high' setting, and cooking from raw, not reheating. A few more quick points:

◐ Check the food really is cooked when you take it out of the microwave.

◐ Remember that most microwave cooking requires

'standing time' after the food is removed from the cooker, to complete the cooking process.

- Bear in mind that the more you put in, the longer it takes to cook. So one jacket potato may take 8 minutes, but two could take 12 minutes or so.
- Remember that if you put a whole egg, in its shell, in the microwave it will explode (I mention this as a warning, not a temptation).

Rule of thumb

If you double the quantity in the recipe or instruction booklet, increase the cooking time by at least 50%.

Food	Mins
Bacon, joint (per lb/400g)	10
Bacon, rashers (2/4/6)	3/5/6
Beef, joint (per lb/400g)	7–8
Cake, fruit (medium-low setting)	40
Cake, sponge	15
Chicken, breast portion	3
Chicken, whole (per lb/400g)	10
Chops (1/2/3)	4/5/6
Eggs, fried	3
Eggs, poached	1
Eggs, scrambled	2
Fish, fillets	3
Fish, flat	3
Fish, round	4
Fish, steaks	5
Fruit, hard (1lb/400g)	8–9
Fruit, soft (1lb/400g)	5

Kidney (per lb/400g)	8
Lamb, joint (per lb/400g)	8–10
Liver (per lb/400g)	8
Pasta dried (8oz/200g)	10
Pasta, fresh	4
Pork, joint (per lb/400g)	10
Potatoes, jacket	8
Prawns, raw	3
Rice	15
Rice pudding	45
Sponge pudding	6
Turkey, whole (per lb/400g)	11
Vegetables, leaf and florets	6
Vegetables, root	8–12

Chef's tip

If you're adapting a recipe for the microwave, shorten the cooking time by 25 percent initially, and see how it goes. Reduce the amount of liquid too, as there is less evaporation in a microwave.

WHAT CAN'T YOU PUT IN A MICROWAVE?

Apart from the obvious things (pets, semtex, large pieces of furniture), there are also a number of materials you might use in the kitchen but can't put in the microwave. So in the absence of a label telling you whether it's microwave friendly, here's what does and doesn't go in the microwave:

Yes	No
Boil-in-the-bags	Conventional oven thermometer
China	Foil (unless the instruction book says it's OK)
Cling film	
Glass ceramic	Freezer bags
Heat-resistant plastic	Glass
Metal	Glue (eg dishes repaired with glue)
Oven glass (eg Pyrex)	
Pottery and stoneware, glazed	Metal-lined containers (unless the instruction book says it's OK)
Roasting bags	
	Paper plates
	Plastic that isn't heat-resistant
	Plates or dishes with metallic paint
	Polystyrene
	Pottery and stoneware, unglazed
	Rubber

You can put greaseproof or kitchen paper in a microwave for a short time, but not recycled kitchen paper (which could contain traces of metal).

Rule of thumb
If plastic containers say they are dishwasher safe, they should also be suitable for the microwave.

Kitchen tips

This is really just a random assortment of favourite tips that I thought might come in handy if you're having trouble getting jelly to turn out, or being driven mad by the garlic smell ingrained in your chopping board.

➻— *Kitchen smells* —☙

◑ Remove cooking smells from your hands with vinegar.
◑ If you have stainless steel taps, or a stainless steel spoon, you can rub your hands over them to get rid of smells like fish, garlic or onions.
◑ Use lemon juice to get the smell of garlic out of your chopping board.
◑ Cut apple is supposed to absorb strong cooking smells. Put a piece in the pan when you're frying fish, or keep an apple cut in half near the cooker.
◑ To get rid of the smell of burnt food, boil a small pan of water with lemon wedges, cloves or cinnamon in it.

➻— *Chopping onions* —☙

To stop onions making you cry when you peel them, here are some suggestions:
◑ Put the onion in the freezer for half an hour first.

- Put it in the microwave for a few seconds first.
- Chop it near cold running water.
- Chop it near to the extractor fan of your cooker.
- Hold a couple of wooden matchsticks between your teeth while cutting the onion.
- Chew on a piece of bread.
- Suck on a spoon.
- Cut the root end off last.

Hot chillis

- If you burn yourself preparing hot chillis, apply olive oil to heal the burn.
- If you eat chillis that are far too hot, the reason is because of the oil in them. Since oil and water don't mix, drinking water is of limited use. You want to absorb the oil. So it's better to eat a piece of bread.

Miscellaneous

- Stop jellies and cold moulds sticking by putting water in the mould and tipping out, without drying it off, before you put the jelly in.
- If you want to make ice in a hurry, fill the tray with warm water. It freezes faster than cold water.
- If your brown sugar goes hard in the jar, put a slice of apple in with it to soften it up again.

Emergency rescue

It happens to the best of us sooner or later. You spend ages sweating over a wonderful meal for your guests and then, at the last minute, something goes horribly wrong. Maybe it's your fault (you burnt the pastry), maybe it's their fault (they forgot to mention they were bringing her mother who's visiting this week), maybe it's no one's fault (the oven is on the blink).

Whatever the cause, right now you just want to know how to remedy it without anyone else noticing. So here are some quick suggestions to help you.

⊶— Cooking disasters —⊷

IT WON'T TURN OUT ⊶━▶

Assuming you've tried standing it in hot water, palette knife round the edge, that sort of thing:

- ◑ Sometimes the container is dispensible and you can make a policy decision to sacrifice the tupperware.
- ◑ Slice the thing up and serve it differently from the way you'd intended.
- ◑ Make a bit of a mess turning it out and then hide this under slices of lemon or whipped cream or whatever is appropriate.

IT WON'T SET ⚫━━◆

If you have time, turn the whole thing out and try again with more gelatine or whatever setting agent you're using. If you haven't time for this, serve the dish up sloppy or runny but make it look intentional. Pour it into individual ramekins to serve, or present your raspberry mousse as raspberry soup (put it in a tureen and garnish it and your guests are guaranteed to believe it was intentional).

IT WON'T RISE ⚫━━◆

You need to be confident here and make out it's supposed to look like this. After all, the taste isn't going to be affected. So just serve your steamed pudding as 'Sussex flat cake' and sound convincing. Unrisen foods can be a bit stodgy so serve it with something light such as whipped cream (whipping it makes it look as if it was deliberate).

IT'S BURNT ⚫━━◆

There are various options depending on how burnt the thing is:

- Discard just the burnt bits and bulk out the rest. For example leave the burnt bits of curry in the bottom of the pan and serve extra rice to make up for it.
- Beef up the taste of the accompaniments to singed food. For example, overly-browned chicken pieces might taste great with caramelised onions.
- Cut off the burnt edges of a cake and ice it to hide the fact.
- Scrape off burnt surfaces of hard foods like crusty bread with a grater.

Chef's tip

If you burn pastry really badly, remove it completely and serve what's underneath in some other way. Replace the lid of a steak and kidney pie with sliced potatoes, or the top of an apple pie with whipped cream or meringue.

IT'S COLLAPSED ▬▬▶

It's going to taste fine; this is just a presentation issue. If the collapse is minimal, hide it with some kind of garnish. If it's substantial, find another way to present it – in individual dishes, chopped up, in a pancake – whatever works and you have the ingredients and equipment for.

IT'S CURDLED ▬▬▶

If custards and sauces curdle, you can generally pass them through a fine sieve or put them in the blender to remix. For cakes and sponges just keep going and it won't show in the finished cake.

Chef's tip

To salvage a split Hollandaise or mayonnaise sauce, start again with fresh egg yolks in the bowl and gradually add the curdled mixture as you would the butter or oil. If you've used your last egg, substitute it with a spoonful of boiling water instead.

It won't defrost ━━●

○ Use a microwave if you have one.

○ Cook it anyway. Just make sure it's well cooked through. You'll get tougher meat but at least it will be ready on time.

○ Speed up the defrosting by putting the thing in something waterproof, such as a plastic bag, and putting it under running cold water.

○ Put it in front of a cold electric fan (no, I don't know why it should work either). Stand it on a metal tray as this will conduct heat better.

○ Cut it into smaller pieces which will thaw out quicker.

○ Serve it frozen. This isn't a good move with raw meat, but a frozen mousse can reasonably be served up and called a parfait.

○ Eat later.

It's dried out ━━●

If your meat has dried out, just make a sauce to go with it (that's what gravy is for). If you're stumped for how to do this fast, boil down double cream until it's reduced to the consistency of a sauce. Add cooking juices, herbs, spices, wine or other flavours to make it tasty.

The timing goes all wrong ━━●

It's such a pain when half your meal is ready and the other half isn't cooked. Here are some ideas to help:

○ Delay the start of the meal. Find something to serve as a starter to make it look deliberate – a packet of crisps or some Bombay mix. Or take a longer break between main course and pudding (it will make you look very relaxed and continental).

○ Put whatever you can in a low oven to keep warm. Put butter on vegetables to stop them drying out.

○ Speed up the thing that isn't ready if you can. For example, take the broccoli off the heat, remove the stems and then put it back on to finish cooking.

○ Abandon it. Difficult with the main course, but a side vegetable that won't play ball won't be missed by anyone but you.

⊶ *Equipment failure* ⊷

A KEY INGREDIENT IS MISSING ⊶

It's gone off, the children ate it without asking, you forgot to buy it... whatever the reason, what do you do when a vital part of your meal isn't there? One of these ideas may help:

○ If the meat is uneatable, serve the same sauce with pasta instead.

○ If the potatoes have gone squishy, serve rice instead.

○ If one vegetable in your casserole or sauce is mouldy, just replace it with something else.

○ If the main flavouring is missing – say the kids ate the chocolate for the mousse – make a lemon mousse instead.

○ If you can't make pastry or crumble because you're out of flour, use a different topping, or even none at all.

YOU FORGOT TO TURN THE OVEN ON ⊶

Ideally just delay the meal. But if one of your lunch guests has to rush off and catch a train or something, start by accepting that you have to change the menu. Then cook the meat or fish or whatever it is in smaller pieces. That will be much quicker. You can either put them in the oven like that, or design a new dish that involves grilling or sautéeing.

EXTRA GUESTS HAVE ARRIVED UNEXPECTEDLY

There are two basic options when you have four chicken breasts between five of you, or six prepared desserts in ramekin dishes and a seventh person arrives without warning:

- ◐ Chop it up – for example, four chicken breasts, each cut into five strips, will serve five people nicely.
- ◐ Pool it – pour those desserts into a one large dish and serve from that. If it looks a mess, cover it with whipped cream or some kind of garnish.

Problem foods

Some foods are just famously difficult to get right. Potatoes and rice are the two most obvious examples of this. Here are a few tips on how to cope when they go wrong.

POTATOES

LUMPY MASHED POTATOES

- ◐ Beat them with a wooden spoon. If that doesn't work, push them through a sieve. If they go cold, reheat them in the serving dish in the oven, with a little butter on the top.

○ Alternatively, fry up some onions and add a sprinkling of rosemary. Put the whole lot through the blender with the potato. It won't remove all the lumps, but it won't show because the onion will be intentionally lumpy too.

ROAST POTATOES THAT WON'T BROWN

Put a bit of butter in with them. It will burn slightly and add colour. Obviously move them up to the top of a hot oven if you can, too. Failing all that, take them out of the oven and deep fry them to finish them off.

BOILED POTATOES THAT BREAK UP

Just mash them instead. If you're boiling them in their skins, squish them with the back of a spoon and serve them as 'crushed potatoes'.

DAUPHINOIS POTATOES

These are those potatoes you slice, cover in either stock or cream, and bake in the oven. You might add onions or cheese. For some reason they frequently take five times longer to cook than your recipe says. If this happens (and you don't have a microwave) drain off any excess liquid and sauté them in a frying pan. Any stray traces of cream or cheese will brown nicely.

RICE ━━●

For how to cook rice so it doesn't burn or stick, see page 81. However, if it's too late for that:

○ Try to salvage sticky rice by putting it in a colander and pouring boiling water through it.

○ Failing that, form it into balls (with a beaten egg if necessary) and fry them. Deep fry them if you have the wherewithal. Then serve them on the side as rice balls.

◐ If the rice is burnt, lay a slice of bread on top of it in the pan. Put a tight fitting lid on the pan and leave for 10 minutes. The bread should absorb much of the burnt taste. Now spoon out the rice that's OK very carefully, discarding anything borderline as it will taste burnt.

Incidentally (brazen plug here) you'll find plenty more where this came from in my book *Recipes for Disasters How to turn kitchen cock-ups into magnificent meals* (White Ladder Press £7.99).

Christmas

This is the time of year when you're just about bound to stretch your capabilities to the limit. The non-cook struggles to come up with a basic roast, while the accomplished chef – not content with breezing through roast turkey with roast potatoes and two veg – attempts to produce half a dozen home made accompaniments along with several elaborate vegetable dishes and a wide choice of puddings and extras. So whatever level your cookery skills are at, this feast calls for all your planning and organisational skills as well. The following checklists, facts and figures should help you create a calm and relaxed Christmas in the kitchen.

Turkey

RECOGNISING GOOD TURKEY

- The breast should be large and full.
- The skin should be unbroken.
- The legs should be smooth.
- The feet should be flexible with a short spur.
- There should be no stickiness.
- Turkey should never smell unpleasant.

COOKING TIME —▶

20 minutes per lb/400g plus 20 minutes. Allow about an extra 30 minutes if you've stuffed the turkey.

COOKING TEMPERATURE —▶

180°C, 350°F, gas mark 4, range cooker baking oven

DEFROSTING TIME —▶

If you buy a frozen turkey, you should defrost it thoroughly before you cook it, for both taste and food safety reasons. Ideally defrost it on the botom shelf of the fridge, though you can put it in cold water (in a watertight bag). It will take longer to defrost than you think. Here's a rough guide to defrosting times:

- ◑ If you're defrosting in the fridge, allow roughly 5–6 hours per lb/10–12 hours per kilo (see, I said it would take longer than you think)
- ◑ If you're defrosting in cold water, allow roughly $1^{1}/_{2}$–2 hours per lb/3–4 hours per kilo

Chef's tip

If your turkey is too big to weigh on the kitchen scales, use the bathroom scales.

CLASSIC ACCOMPANIMENTS —▶

- ◑ Cranberry sauce
- ◑ Bread sauce
- ◑ Stuffing
- ◑ Chipolata sausages

How many will it feed? ➖➤

There's a really convenient rule of thumb here: allow 1lb/400g turkey per person.

How can you tell when it's cooked?

Pierce the thickest part of the leg. If the juices run clear, with no trace of blood, the turkey is cooked. If you have a meat thermometer, the internal temperature should read at least 72°C.

How to carve a roast turkey ➖➤

After resting the bird for about 10 minutes, put it on a board breast side up.

- ❍ Remove one of the drumsticks. If you're being fancy rather than rustic you now slice the meat from the drumstick.
- ❍ Staying on the same side of the turkey, you now slice the meat from the thigh.
- ❍ Remove the wing and cut the meat from it (slicing might be a bit of a tall order by this point).
- ❍ Still on the same side, slice the breast thinly lengthwise.
- ❍ Repeat all this on the other side.

➖ *Goose* ➖

Recognising good goose ➖➤

- ❍ The breast should be plump.
- ❍ The lower back should be flexible.

◐ There should be no stickiness.
◐ Goose should never smell unpleasant.

APPROXIMATE COOKING TIME

20 minutes per lb/400g plus 20 minutes. Allow about an extra 30 minutes if the goose is stuffed.

COOKING TEMPERATURE

220°C, 425°F, gas mark 7, range cooker floor of roasting oven

CLASSIC ACCOMPANIMENTS

◐ Apple or gooseberry sauce
◐ Sage and onion stuffing

HOW MANY WILL IT FEED?

Allow $1^1/_2$lb/750g per person as goose has a high ratio of bone to meat.

HOW CAN YOU TELL WHEN IT'S COOKED?

Pierce the thickest part of the leg. If the juices run clear, with no trace of blood, you've cooked your goose. If you have a meat thermometer, the internal temperature should read at least 72°C.

HOW TO CARVE A ROAST GOOSE

After resting the bird for about 10 minutes, stand it on a board with the breast side up.
◐ Remove the legs and wings first.

◑ Carve thick slices of meat from the whole length of the breast.

Chef's tip

Remember to keep draining off the fat when roasting goose. It's the best fat for roasting potatoes and any you don't use can be stored in the fridge in a screw-top jar.

❧— *Gammon* —❧

A home cooked gammon makes a wonderful traditional Christmas breakfast, and goes well with cold turkey on Boxing Day as well. You can buy it, of course, but then you'd miss out on the delicious cooking smells which, for me, really signify that it's Christmas Eve.

Gammon usually needs soaking for several hours (overnight is a good idea) to reduce its saltiness. Once you've cooked the ham there are lots of recipes for glazing it, but essentially you just need to coat it in something sweet, such as brown sugar or honey, and either spike it with cloves or add some other Christmas spice to the sugar or honey.

APPROXIMATE COOKING TIME ●——▶

Boiling 20 minutes per lb/400g plus 20 minutes. For a gammon over about 6lbs/3kg reduce this to 15 minutes per lb/400g plus 15 minutes.

Roasting 25 minutes per lb/400g plus 25 minutes.

COOKING TEMPERATURE ➟

Roasting 180°C, 350°F, gas mark 4–5, range cooker baking oven

✎ *Chef's tip*

It's often recommended that you boil the gammon for the first half of the cooking time, and then transfer it to the oven and bake it. This keeps it moist and retains maximum flavour.

CLASSIC ACCOMPANIMENTS ➟

- ◑ Mustard
- ◑ Chutney

HOW MANY WILL IT FEED? ➟

If it's your main dish (rather than a light breakfast or one of several cold meats on offer) you should allow an uncooked weight of:

- ◑ 10oz/300g per person for gammon on the bone
- ◑ 8oz/250g if you're cooking a boned joint

➟ *Planning checklist* ➟

In the run up to Christmas it's easy to find yourself fretting that you've forgotten something essential. So here's a checklist of all the standard essentials. Obviously I can't help if your family traditionally celebrates Christmas with baked haddock or jelly and ice cream, but this covers all the standard Christmas fare:

Turkey	*Goose*
Turkey	Goose
Chipolatas	Stuffing
Bacon	Apple sauce
Stuffing	Potatoes
Cranberry sauce	Vegetables
Bread sauce	
Potatoes	
Brussels sprouts	
Other vegetables	

Pudding	*Extras*
Christmas pudding	Gammon
Brandy or rum butter	Christmas cake
Custard	Mince pies
Cream	Wine and spirits
Ice cream	

Chef's tip

If you can't fit everything in the fridge, use it for any meat, fish and milk products. Vegetables and drinks can be kept outside in an unheated garage or shed. A tin with a lid (such as a cake tin) should keep out mice, cats and any other pests. Eggs and cheese can be stored at room temperature.

Countdown

About the toughest part of the whole Christmas dinner is getting everything ready at the same time. So here's a countdown to the meal to help you get everything going at the right time. Obviously without your particular menu in front of me I've gone for standard vegetables and accompaniments, but you should be able to adapt this very easily to your own meal.

Dishing up time minus...	To do
Approx 24 hours	• Remove anything you've frozen ahead from the freezer and transfer it to the fridge. • Prepare vegetables (apart from potatoes).
4 hours (or whatever time you calculate)	• Put the turkey or goose in the oven.
2 hours	• Parboil the potatoes.
1 hour 45 minutes	• Get all the cold sauces and accompaniments ready. • Organise your serving dishes. • Lay the table.
1 hour 15 minutes	• Put the roast potatoes in the oven.
1 hour	• Put any other roast vegetables in the oven. • Turn the potatoes. • Put the pudding on to steam.
45 minutes	• Put the sausages in the oven. • If you're cooking the stuffing separately from the bird, put it in the oven.
25 minutes	• Put water on to boil for vegetables. • Turn the roast potatoes. • Take the turkey or goose out

	of the oven to rest well covered in foil.
20 minutes	• Put sprouts and other green vegetables on.
15 minutes	• Take the roast vegetables out of the oven, transfer to serving dishes and put in oven to keep warm. • Put the sausages in a serving dish and keep warm. • Warm the plates.
10 minutes	• Carve the turkey. • Heat the bread sauce. • Finish the gravy.
0 minutes	• Serve the meal.

Vegetarian alternatives to nut roast

Nut roast is something of a cliché as a vegetarian alternative. If most of your guests are happy to tuck into turkey and you have just one or two vegetarians, you may choose to buy a ready-made vegetarian meal for them. If, however, you want to produce a home made vegetarian dish as well, here are some quick and simple ideas:

◐ Line a flan dish with overlapping sheets of filo pastry and bake blind (following the instructions on the packet). You can do this ahead of the meal. Fill the flan case with any combination you like of cooked vegetables, cheese and nuts – for example chunks of pre-roasted butternut squash and sweet potato, blue cheese and chestnuts. Sprinkle this with parmesan and cook for about 15 minutes in a low to moderate oven.

◐ Make a risotto by adding spices (such as cardamom, cumin or ginger) and herbs (eg coriander or parsley) to the rice, along with pine kernels or nuts, some lemon zest, and finely chopped or shredded vegetables (Brussels sprouts, onions, garlic, celery, mushrooms).

◐ Serve pasta with a tasty but simple sauce. While you're cooking the pasta, fry together some onions, mushrooms and garlic. Add half a pint of double cream and reduce to the consistency of a thick sauce. Throw in some chopped herbs and peeled chestnuts (you can buy them vacuum packed) and pour the sauce over the pasta.

AND TO MAKE THE MAIN MEAL AS VEGETARIAN AS POSSIBLE: ●▬▶

◐ Don't use the fat from the meat to roast potatoes and other vegetables. Use a vegetable oil of some kind. That way your vegetarian guests will be able to eat them.

◐ Likewise, make a non-meat stuffing and cook it separately from the meat.

◐ Use vegetarian suet in the Christmas pudding.

What you can prepare ahead of time

TRIMMINGS ●▬▶

The trick with Christmas is to get as much of the cooking done as you can ahead of Christmas Day itself. You can cook most of the trimmings in advance and freeze them (assuming you don't want to buy them), including:

◐ stuffings

◐ bread sauce, or at least make the breadcrumbs in advance and freeze them

◐ cranberry sauce

◐ apple sauce (for goose)

You can transfer them from the freezer to the fridge on Christmas Eve. I've never tried freezing brandy or rum butter, but I fancy it would mess with the texture. You can however make it several days ahead and keep it in the fridge.

Chef's tip

Current health and safety advice is that you shouldn't cook the stuffing inside the turkey as it may not cook through fully (unless you overcook the turkey). The alternative is to cook it in the same oven as the turkey (if it will fit) for about an hour.

VEGETABLES

You can prepare most vegetables such as carrots and Brussels sprouts on Christmas Eve and keep them in the fridge. Potatoes and parsnips will need to be kept in water of course, to stop them going brown, and are better left to Christmas Day itself.

MINCE PIES

These will keep for several days in a tin, of course. But if you're short of space, or you think you may run out, make up a batch of pastry a few days before Christmas and keep it in the fridge. Making mince pies is really quick if you don't have to make the pastry first. Obviously the alternative is to use ready-made pastry.

❧ *Using up the leftovers* ❧

For some reason it's traditional to buy a turkey that's far too big and then spend the next week eating it. I guess after the cooking marathon of Christmas day it saves you having to cook anything else much for the next few days. If you're so exhausted/full up/hungover that you can't think what to make with the leftovers, here are a few ideas:

- turkey salad
- coronation turkey
- turkey sandwiches (you can use fancy bread to pep it up)
- turkey curry
- turkey risotto
- pasta sauce (make a white sauce and add cooked turkey plus any flavourings you like such as onion, lemon zest and herbs)
- turkey soup

The current advice is that you should take cold meat off the bone and keep it in the fridge, for no more than two days.

- **Brussels sprouts**, despite not being the world's most popular vegetable, do make the very best bubble & squeak. As good a brunch on Boxing Day as you could ask for, with a bit of cold turkey or ham.
- **Christmas pudding** can be reheated quickly by slic-

ing and frying it in butter. OK it's not the most slimming of foods, but by this stage of Christmas it's probably too late to worry about that anyway.

Rule of thumb

Cooked food should be reheated only once, and should be hot right through.

Classic recipes you need to check

There are certain things you cook frequently, and you know perfectly well how to cook them, but somehow when it comes to it you can't quite remember the quantities or proportions involved. After consulting dozens of people who regularly cook, I've identified the top dozen recipes that most commonly fall into this category.

So if you can never quite remember whether it's half a pint or one pint of milk to 4oz of flour – or whatever – the quantities below should serve as a quick reminder. I have mostly not included how to make the thing as you know that perfectly well already, though in one or two cases I've added a line or two that I think may help.

I should just add that in some cases there is more than one standard recipe (if that's not a contradiction in terms). You may find alternative versions elsewhere, but the one below will serve you as well as any.

BATTER/PANCAKE/YORKSHIRE PUDDING MIX

4oz/100g flour
pinch salt
1 egg
$^1/_2$ pint/250ml milk

BREAD

$1^1/_2$lb/700g strong plain flour
2 tspn salt
$^1/_2$ oz/10g lard
$^1/_2$ pint/375ml water
$^1/_2$ oz/10g fresh yeast, or $1^1/_2$ tspn quick dried yeast with
1 tspn caster sugar

BUTTER CREAM/BUTTER ICING

8oz/200g butter
6oz/150g icing sugar

CAKE MIXTURE

Obviously there are loads of different cake recipes, but for
your bog standard Victoria sandwich cake the quantities
are 4/4/4/2 (that's the easiest way to remember it):

4oz butter
4oz sugar
4oz flour
2 eggs

Of course if you insist on working in metric it's not
quite such an easy mnemonic, as it becomes 100g/100g/
100g/2.

CHEESE SAUCE

1oz/25g butter
1oz/25g flour
$^1/_2$ pint milk

2oz/50g grated cheese (officially, but actually as much as
you like, and the milder the cheese the more you'll need).
I have been asked several times to include in this book a
way of making white sauce and cheese sauce without all

that bloody stirring. Well, I'm afraid you do have to do more stirring than you'd like but, if you warm the milk before you add it, you'll reduce the time you spend slaving over the stove.

CRUMBLE TOPPING

The basic proportions to remember are 6/4/2:

6oz/150g plain flour
4oz/100g butter
2oz/50g sugar

Incidentally, these are the same quantities for shortbread biscuits, although the texture is different. That's just because with crumble you create a breadcrumby texture with the butter and flour and then stir in the sugar. With the biscuits you combine all the ingredients into more of a paste.

GRAVY

I'm not sure this really belongs in this section as it is more of a recipe than a reminder of quantities. However, so many people asked for it that here it is.

If you want to thicken gravy, you need to use about a dessertspoonful of fat from the roasting pan and a dessertspoonful of flour for every 4–6 people.

Make a roux by cooking these together, and then add the roasting juices, after removing any additional fat. If this doesn't give you enough liquid, add either stock or the water from cooking the vegetables. This liquid should first be used to deglaze the roasting pan.

Alternatively, if you can skim off all but your dessert-spoonful of fat without removing the roasting juices from the roasting pan, you can make the gravy in the pan by sprinkling the flour over it and leaving it for a few minutes to absorb the remaining fat. Stir it all in and get the lumps out, then add the stock or vegetable water until you have the right consistency.

ICE CREAM MIX/CUSTARD

The basic plain ice cream recipe is also, before you add the cream, the recipe for a traditional egg custard sauce, should you be one of the increasingly rare people who actually makes their own custard. There are many recipes for ice cream of course, but this is the most basic, to which you can add flavourings as you choose.

4 egg yolks
4oz/100g caster sugar
$1/_2$ pint milk
$1/_2$ pint cream

MERINGUES

These follow on happily from ice cream, as they give you something to do with the left over egg whites.

4 egg whites
8oz/200g caster sugar

PIZZA BASE

These quantities will make two 9-inch pizza bases.

8oz strong plain flour
$1/_2$ tspn salt
$1/_2$ tspn quick, dried yeast
$1/_2$ pint/125ml warm water
1 tblspn olive oil

RICE PUDDING

The following quantities are generally said to serve 4, but it's my experience that most people will happily eat more, so err on the generous side.

2oz/50g short grain rice
2oz/50g caster sugar
1 pint/500ml milk
butter to dot on the top

Remember that rice pudding always takes longer to cook than you think.

ROYAL ICING

1lb/400g icing sugar
3 egg whites
juice of 1 lemon
2 tspns glycerine

SHORTCRUST PASTRY

Twice as much flour to fat, by weight. So for standard quantities:

8oz/200g flour
4oz/100g fat

You can use half lard/half butter or, for a really light pastry, all lard. To keep it crumbly, use the least water you can get away with, generally about 3–4 tablespoons for the quantities above.

WATER ICING/GLACÉ ICING

8oz/200g icing sugar
2 tblspns warm water or other liquid (lemon juice, orange juice or whatever you please)

WHITE SAUCE

1oz/25g butter
1oz/25g flour
$^1/_2$ pint milk

Some people, eager to minimise the stirring involved, make white sauce using simply cornflour and milk. This certainly makes a sauce, and it is indeed white. However it lacks the flavour of a true white sauce. You have to make the choice between more effort + more flavour, or less effort + less flavour.

Contact us

You're welcome to contact White Ladder Press if you have any questions or comments for either us or the author. Please use whichever of the following routes suits you.

Phone: 01803 813343

Email: enquiries@whiteladderpress.com

Fax: 01803 813928

Address: White Ladder Press, Great Ambrook, Near Ipplepen, Devon TQ12 5UL

Website: www.whiteladderpress.com

What can our website do for you?

If you want more information about any of our books, you'll find it at **www.whiteladderpress.com**. In particular you'll find extracts from each of our books, and reviews of those that are already published. We also run special offers on future titles if you order online before publication. And you can request a copy of our free catalogue.

Many of our books also have links pages, useful addresses and so on relevant to the subject of the book. You can find out a bit more about us and, if you're a writer yourself, you'll find our submission guidelines for authors. So please check us out and let us know if you have any comments, questions or suggestions.

The GARDENER'S POCKET BIBLE

EVERY GARDENING RULE OF THUMB
at your fingertips

Do you know every gardening technique and rule of thumb off pat? Or do you occasionally straighten up from your digging to try and remember exactly what you're meant to be doing? How deep should you plant these bulbs? Was it now you were supposed to prune this rose, or in February? Can you compost this weed? Is it OK to plant out these seedlings now?

It's such a pain having to go indoors, kick off your boots, shed your outdoor clothes and start looking up the answer to your question in some great gardening tome. And that's where *The Gardener's Pocket Bible* comes in. Because now, you can stay in the garden and look up all those essential facts and figures in an instant. At your fingertips you'll have all the answers to your on-the-spot questions such as:

- Which plants do you need to protect from frost?
- When should you cut the hedge?
- What plants need staking, and when?
- How can you get rid of greenfly without using pesticides?

This indispensible little guide will tell you what you need to know, when you need to know it – and will save you thumbing through gardening encyclopedias when what you actually want to do is get on with the gardening.

£7.99

Recipes *for* Disaster~s~

How to turn kitchen cock-ups into magnificent meals

"Methinks 'twould have spared me much grief had I had this cunning volume to hand when I burnt those cursèd cakes." *King Alfred the Great*

It was all going so well… friends for lunch, guests for dinner, family for Christmas. You're planning a delicious meal, relaxed yet sophisticated, over which everyone can chat, drink a glass of fine wine and congratulate you on your culinary talent.

And then, just as you were starting to enjoy it – disaster! The pastry has burnt, the pudding has collapsed or the terrine won't turn out. Or the main ingredient has been eaten by the cat. Or perhaps it's the guests who've buggered everything up: they forgot to mention that they're vegetarian (you've made a beef bourguignon). Or they've brought along a friend (you've only made six crème brûlées).

But don't panic. There are few kitchen cock-ups that can't be successfully salvaged if you know how. With the right attitude you are no longer accident-prone, but adaptable. Not a panicker but a creative, inspirational cook. Recipes for Disasters is packed with useful tips and ideas for making sure that your entertaining always runs smoothly (or at least appears to, whatever is going on behind the scenes). Yes, you still can have a reputation as a culinary paragon, even if it is all bluff.

£7.99

Index